FOURTH EDITION

# JOURNALISM TODAY!

## WORKBOOK

DONALD L. FERGUSON

JIM PATTEN

## National Textbook Company

*a division of* NTC/CONTEMPORARY PUBLISHING COMPANY
Lincolnwood, Illinois USA

*Cover design*
Ophelia M. Chambliss

*Cover photo credits*

Left: The Bettman Archive

Top right: Jeff Ellis

Middle right: Jeff Ellis, with permission of the *Chicago Sun-Times*

Bottom right: © 1993, *Chicago Tribune*

# ACKNOWLEDGMENTS

The publisher and authors wish to thank the following journalism instructors and advisers for their contributions to the development of this edition of the *Journalism Today! Workbook*:

Barbara Markelz, Joliet (Ill.) Township High School, West Campus
Leslie J. Nicholas, Wyoming Valley West High School, Plymouth, Pa.
Candace Perkins, St. Charles (Ill.) High School.

Grateful acknowledgment is also made to the following:

Associated Press News Features, New York, N.Y.
*The Advocate*, Mayo High School, Rochester, Minn.
*The Arizona Daily Star* (Tucson, Ariz.)
*The Bear Facts*, Lake Braddock Secondary School, Burke, Va.
*Cedar Rapids Gazette* (Cedar Rapids, Iowa)
*Des Moines Register* (Des Moines, Iowa)
*The Hoof Print*, Alamo Heights High School, San Antonio, Texas
Joliet (Ill.) Township High School, West Campus, *Yearbook*
National Scholastic Press Association, Minneapolis, Minn.
*The Oracle*, North High School, Des Moines, Iowa
*The Railsplitter*, Lincoln High School, Des Moines, Iowa
*The Rampage*, Rockville (Md.) High School
*The Rustler*, Fremont (Neb.) Senior High School
*The Scroll*, East High School, Des Moines, Iowa
*The Scroll*, Sunset High School, Beaverton, Ore.
*silver chips*, Montgomery Blair High School, Silver Springs, Md.
*The Statesman*, John Jay High School, San Antonio, Texas
*The Torch*, Wichita (Kan.) High School South
United Press International, Washington, D.C.
*valor/dictus*, James W. Robinson High School, Fairfax, Va.
*The X-Ray*, St. Charles (Ill.) High School

Special thanks also go to the following for their contributions and assistance: Murray Butler, Karen Kehr, Annette Kerstan, Patrick Laconovi, Allin Means, Wendy Prater, and Adrian Vaughan, all of Baylor University, Waco, Texas; Mike Gaughan, Columbine High School, Aurora, Colo.; and Bobby Hawthorne, Interscholastic League Press Conference.

**Note**

The Code of Ethics in Chapter 1 is reprinted by permission of the National Ethics Committee of the Society of Professional Journalists. Copies of their *Freedom of Information Report*, published annually, can be ordered at $1.00 per copy from SPJ, PO Box 77, 16 S. Jackson, Greencastle, Ind. 46135.

The NCEW's Basic Statement of Principles included in Chapter 10 is reprinted by permission of the National Council of Editorial Writers. Copies of their brochure *So You Want to Know About Editorial Writers: Some Questions and Answers* can be ordered through the NCEW, 6223 Executive Blvd., Rockville, Md. 20852.

# CONTENTS

INTRODUCTION     vii

**Chapter 1**

CONSIDERING LAW AND ETHICS     1

**Chapter 2**

WORKING ON NEWS JUDGMENT     9

**Chapter 3**

DOING INTERVIEWS     16

**Chapter 4**

WRITING LEADS     23

**Chapter 5**

WRITING NEWS STORIES     33

**Chapter 6**

USING QUOTES     56

**Chapter 7**

COVERING SPEECHES     67

**Chapter 8**

WRITING FEATURE STORIES     74

**Chapter 9**

WRITING SPORTS STORIES 85

**Chapter 10**

WRITING EDITORIALS 101

**Chapter 11**

WRITING HEADLINES AND DOING LAYOUT 110

**Chapter 12**

USING PHOTOS EFFECTIVELY 126

**Chapter 13**

CREATING ADS 133

**Chapter 14**

PLANNING THE YEARBOOK 139

**Chapter 15**

WRITING FOR BROADCAST 148

**Appendix A**

BRAINSTORMING TECHNIQUE 157

**Appendix B**

COPY EDITING SYMBOLS 159

# INTRODUCTION

Even if you have a natural writing talent and a curiosity about people and the way things work, you still need to practice to develop your skills and become an effective journalist. Through carefully sequenced activities, the *Journalism Today! Workbook* offers you that practice.

The opening chapter of the *Journalism Today! Workbook* deals with law and ethics. From the first day of class, you should be aware that the law applies to student journalists, too. In the past students have been sued. One aim here is to prevent future lawsuits.

Chapters 2–11 cover a full range of journalistic functions. They include a variety of exercises carefully selected to emphasize the basics of good writing, story construction, style, editing and layout. Chapters 12–15 provide practical hands-on experience in the use of photographs, preparing advertising and yearbook copy and design, and adapting of writing to broadcasting. Appendix A is a section on a brainstorming technique you can use to stimulate creative thinking and come up with story ideas. Appendix B is a chart of copy editing symbols for your reference as you practice editing.

Each chapter in the *Journalism Today! Workbook* begins with a capsule summary of material from the *Journalism Today!* textbook. Exercises follow. Write-in space is provided for exercises, but you may choose to use separate paper for activities that require more writing.

A journalist has simple goals: to inform, entertain, and in the case of editorials, to persuade readers, listeners, or viewers. As a journalism student, you will learn good taste, news judgment and responsibility. Equally important, you will learn to determine what is *news*, how to master the writing of effective stories and how to handle layout, photography, advertising and yearbook design.

Journalism is an exciting field of study and an exciting career. To be a successful journalist, you must have the dedication to write and continually improve your skills and knowledge—both as a student and throughout your career.

Donald L. Ferguson
Jim Patten

# CONSIDERING LAW AND ETHICS

Journalists in free, open societies have tremendous freedom. Censorship is rare—and almost always illegal. The president can't tell the White House press corps what to write (although he might like to); the mayor can't tell the City Hall reporter what to write (although she might like to). It is not, therefore, the government that regulates what journalists do. Journalists regulate themselves, for the most part, because their freedom is guaranteed by the First Amendment to the Constitution.

But, free or not, journalists subscribe to strict rules they have developed over the years. Journalists try to be objective. That means they report facts, and they do not let their own feelings or opinions interfere with the reporting. They seek balance, meaning they tell both (or all) sides in controversial situations. They avoid conflict-of-interest situations, such as reporting on issues about which they have feelings too strong to permit them to be objective. They treat all segments of society the same, not favoring any group because of gender, age, race or economic status—or for any other reason. They try to be fair, neutral, honest. The normal ethics most humans believe in are etched in stone in the newsroom.

Journalists put a great deal of emphasis on good taste, trying hard to stay away from material that may offend audiences unnecessarily. They open their columns and airwaves to dissenting opinions, recognizing their obligation to function as a forum for all ideas.

In a scholastic situation, journalists generally are free to report accurately what they see fit except for four major areas: libel, invasion of privacy, obscenity and substantial disruption.

*Libel* is an incredibly intricate area of the law. Vastly simplified, the rules are as follows. Libel is false defamation; that is, it is material that reduces the reputation of another (defames him/her), and it is false. No one may publish a libel legally. That just means journalists cannot legally print or air lies about other people—either on purpose or accidentally. They cannot suggest that someone is of low moral character or is a thief or cheat or has a loathsome disease. They cannot print that which would cause others to shun the offended person. If they do, and if what they print is not true, they can be penalized.

The penalty is money. The loser pays the winner, and the judgments can run into hundreds of thousands of dollars. Occasionally the judgments reach into the millions. So be super wary in any situation in which a story might reduce anyone's reputation. (But don't get fanatic about it. It is not libelous to say "She struck out with the bases loaded," even if that might "reduce her reputation." Journalists can almost always print what is true.)

*Invasion of privacy* is against the law. Your common sense will work here. You cannot force your way into someone's home to take a picture or climb over their back fence. This is called intrusion, and it is one of four areas in invasion of privacy.

Another is called false light, and it usually involves photos, too. Do not print a photo of someone in an innocent situation and then, in the caption, suggest that something non-innocent happened. For example, you cannot photograph a mother scolding her child and run the photo to illustrate a series on child abuse. Scolding isn't abusing, so that would be placing her in a false light.

Another area of privacy is called disclosure of embarrassing private facts, which usually involves old criminal charges. For example, it would be an invasion of privacy if you were to write that 45 years ago, the president of a furniture store in your town was found guilty of shoplifting. If the merchant had led an exemplary life those 45 years, it would be senseless, obviously, to dredge up the old scandal. (You would win if he sued for libel because truth is an absolute defense; but you would lose a right to privacy suit.)

The final area of privacy is called appropriation, and it means you cannot appropriate another person's name or likeness for commercial gain. Thus it is against the law to open a clothing store called Oprah Winfrey's Clothing Shoppe unless you are Oprah Winfrey. She owns her name and you cannot appropriate it. The same is true of her likeness. You cannot photograph another person and use that photo for your own commercial profit. You can photograph anyone in a newsworthy situation and print the photo. But do it right.

*Obscenity*, another restricted area, also is complicated. The courts have been struggling for years to define what is and what is not obscene. In fact, for journalistic purposes on the scholastic level, the definition doesn't matter a great deal. A simple test would be to ask if the material in question would be offensive to the audience. If the answer is "yes" or "maybe," leave it out.

*Substantial disruption* is the element that forbids scholastic journalists from printing or airing material that would cause the normal educational functions to stop or be seriously impaired. A simple example would be an editorial urging students to burn their books and to march on the school's administration offices. Since such action would disrupt education, school administrators, according to the latest Supreme Court ruling, have the *right* to deny publication of such an editorial. (Specifically, in 1988 the *Hazelwood School District v. Kuhlmeier* case came up before the Supreme Court. In the ruling handed down, the Supreme Court stipulated that school administrators may exercise "editorial control over the style and content of speech in school activities," including student publications.)

It should also be noted that broadcast journalists operate under different regulations. Whereas for the most part the government plays little or no role in regulating print journalists, it does play a role in regulating broadcast journalists. This is because the airwaves belong to all of us, collectively, as a nation. And the airwaves are limited. There is no limit to the number of newspapers that are printed in the U.S., but there is a limit on the number of airwaves available to TV and radio stations for broadcast. So the government regulates broadcast frequencies, not permitting two stations in the same region to use the same frequency. The government also regulates broadcast media by requiring equal time and equal access for political candidates. Stations must give candidates equal time on the air (although not necessarily on news shows) and must sell commercial air time to all candidates who want to buy it.

## Exercise 1

Read the Society of Professional Journalists' Code of Ethics on page 4. Write your opinion for the following questions.

a. How is the Code of Ethics intended to be enforced?

_____

_____

_____

b. What are the benefits of ''voluntary'' enforcement?

_____

_____

_____

_____

c. What are the weaknesses of a ''voluntary'' approach?

_____

_____

_____

(Questions continue on page 5)

**Society of Professional Journalists**

# Code of Ethics

SOCIETY of Professional Journalists believes the duty of journalists is to serve the truth.

We BELIEVE the agencies of mass communication are carriers of public discussion and information, acting on their Constitutional mandate and freedom to learn and report the facts.

We BELIEVE in public enlightenment as the forerunner of justice, and in our Constitutional role to seek the truth as part of the public's right to know the truth.

We BELIEVE those responsibilities carry obligations that require journalists to perform with intelligence, objectivity, accuracy, and fairness.

To these ends, we declare acceptance of the standards of practice here set forth:

## I. RESPONSIBILITY:

The public's right to know of events of public importance and interest is the overriding mission of the mass media. The purpose of distributing news and enlightened opinion is to serve the general welfare. Journalists who use their professional status as representatives of the public for selfish or other unworthy motives violate a high trust.

## II. FREEDOM OF THE PRESS:

Freedom of the press is to be guarded as an inalienable right of people in a free society. It carries with it the freedom and the responsibility to discuss, question, and challenge actions and utterances of our government and of our public and private institutions. Journalists uphold the right to speak unpopular opinions and the privilege to agree with the majority.

## III. ETHICS:

Journalists must be free of obligation to any interest other than the public's right to know the truth.

1. Gifts, favors, free travel, special treatment or privileges can compromise the integrity of journalists and their employers. Nothing of value should be accepted.

2. Secondary employment, political involvement, holding public office, and service in community organizations should be avoided if it compromises the integrity of journalists and their employers. Journalists and their employers should conduct their personal lives in a manner that protects them from conflict of interest, real or apparent. Their responsibilities to the public are paramount. That is the nature of their profession.

3. So-called news communications from private sources should not be published or broadcast without substantiation of their claims to news values.

4. Journalists will seek news that serves the public interest, despite the obstacles. They will make constant efforts to assure that the public's business is conducted in public and that public records are open to public inspection.

5. Journalists acknowledge the newsman's ethic of protecting confidential sources of information.

6. Plagiarism is dishonest and unacceptable.

## IV. ACCURACY AND OBJECTIVITY:

Good faith with the public is the foundation of all worthy journalism.

1. Truth is our ultimate goal.

2. Objectivity in reporting the news is another goal that serves as the mark of an experienced professional. It is a standard of performance toward which we strive. We honor those who achieve it.

3. There is no excuse for inaccuracies or lack of thoroughness.

4. Newspaper headlines should be fully warranted by the contents of the articles they accompany. Photographs and telecasts should give an accurate picture of an event and not highlight an incident out of context.

5. Sound practice makes clear distinction between news reports and expressions of opinion. News reports should be free of opinion or bias and represent all sides of an issue.

6. Partisanship in editorial comment that knowingly departs from the truth violates the spirit of American journalism.

7. Journalists recognize their responsibility for offering informed analysis, comment, and editorial opinion on public events and issues. They accept the obligation to present such material by individuals whose competence, experience, and judgment qualify them for it.

8. Special articles or presentations devoted to advocacy or the writer's own conclusions and interpretations should be labeled as such.

## V. FAIR PLAY:

Journalists at all times will show respect for the dignity, privacy, rights, and well-being of people encountered in the course of gathering and presenting the news.

1. The news media should not communicate unofficial charges affecting reputation or moral character without giving the accused a chance to reply.

2. The news media must guard against invading a person's right to privacy.

3. The media should not pander to morbid curiosity about details of vice and crime.

4. It is the duty of news media to make prompt and complete correction of their errors.

5. Journalists should be accountable to the public for their reports and the public should be encouraged to voice its grievances against the media. Open dialogue with our readers, viewers, and listeners should be fostered.

## VI. MUTUAL TRUST:

Adherence to this code is intended to preserve and strengthen the bond of mutual trust and respect between American journalists and the American people.

The Society shall--by programs of education and other means--encourage individual journalists to adhere to these tenets, and shall encourage journalistic publications and broadcasters to recognize their responsibility to frame codes of ethics in concert with their employees to serve as guidelines in furthering these goals.

**CODE OF ETHICS**
(Adopted 1926; revised 1973, 1984, 1987)

d. Are there benefits to a code of ethics that cannot be enforced by censuring or expelling those who would violate it? Explain.

_____

_____

_____

_____

_____

e. Ethically speaking, can a journalist accept free tickets to an event and fairly write a review about it?

_____

_____

_____

_____

_____

## Exercise 2

Journalists often have to make quick judgments about legal and ethical questions. Here are some to consider.

a. Let's say you're the sports editor of the school paper. You also are on the basketball team. Should you write the news stories about the basketball team?

_____

_____

_____

_____

b. The Board of Education in your town is considering whether to ask the people to approve a bond issue to build a new school. The new school would cost several million dollars. You're a reporter for your school paper and you're assigned to cover the board meeting on the evening the board decides on the issue. During the meeting, the president of the board says to you, "I'm sorry, but this meeting is closed to the press. I must ask you to leave." What should you do?

_____

_____

_____

_____

_____

c. You're a reporter for your school paper, and you are interviewing a faculty member. In response to a question, the faculty member offers to give you an answer only if it's off the record. What should you do?

_____

_____

_____

_____

d. In a report on a Student Council meeting, the student newspaper reports that Student A voted against a resolution. When the story appears, Student A comes to the journalism office and says she did not vote against the resolution. She says that in fact she voted for it. What should the newspaper do?

_____

_____

_____

e. A rock group stages a concert in your town, and a reporter for the school paper writes a review. The review is very critical and negative, saying that the performers were untalented and that the show was a waste of time and money for those attending. Angered, the musicians sue the paper for libel. Who would win this case?

_____

_____

_____

_____

f. In conducting research for an editorial, you read a national magazine article about the topic. One paragraph of the article appeals to you so you insert it in your editorial without credit to the magazine. Your journalism adviser tells you that you have flunked the journalism class. What do you think of this situation?

_____

_____

_____

_____

_____

g. You are a sportswriter for the school paper. After a hard-fought, close football game that your school loses, you interview the football coach. He is angry about the loss, and in your interview uses profanity. Should you quote him?

_____

_____

_____

_____

_____

h. You are a reporter for the school paper. An assistant principal asks to see you. He says he is resigning to go into private business. During the conversation, he is extremely critical of the principal, and he says he is resigning because he cannot stand to work for her any longer. He says she is incompetent and ''shouldn't be allowed to continue as principal.'' You write a story and hand it in. The editor gives it back and tells you, ''This story isn't finished.'' Why did the editor say that?

_____

_____

_____

_____

i. You are a reporter for the school paper. You are interviewing the coaches and football players in the locker room just after an important game that your school lost. The coaches and team members were bitter and disappointed. They said things that they ordinarily would not say. You have been taught to quote people frequently because that is an aid for the reader. What should you do in this situation?

_____

_____

_____

## Exercise 3

With the help of your classmates and teacher, create a code of ethics that you and the whole class can follow. Your code of ethics should cover items relevant in your school. For example, if a teacher you do not like wins the Best Teacher Award, should you write the news story, or should you have someone else write it? Should you accept concert tickets from an athlete who wants a story written about her? If you wish, you can refer to the Code of Ethics on page 4 as your guide.

_____

_____

_____

_____

_____

_____

_____

_____

_____

_____

_____

_____

# WORKING ON NEWS JUDGMENT

Journalists need many skills. Among the critical ones is news judgment, the ability to recognize why one story is more newsworthy than another or why one element within a story is more newsworthy than another. Acquiring good news judgment is best achieved through experience. But some guidelines have been developed that can help get an inexperienced student started.

Stories are said to be newsworthy if they contain one or more of the following *elements* of news: timeliness, proximity, prominence, consequence, human interest and conflict. A story with timeliness is about today, not last year. If the story is to have proximity, it must be about something close to home. The element of prominence involves well-known people, places, or things. Consequence is an element present in, for example, a story about how an international event has affected your community. Human interest is an element in a story about an unusual incident or experience that evokes emotion and is interesting to people in general. Conflict is an element present in stories about war and the struggle for peace, in political stories, sport stories, and in all stories where people are at odds—from City Hall to the United Nations.

Geography, the calendar and competition play a role, too, in determining newsworthiness. Stories about oil prices are more important in Texas than in South Dakota. Stories about preserving water are more important to Arizona than in Washington state. Stories about football are more important in the fall than in the summer. Stories about taxes take on special meaning around April 15. A story is better if the opposition newspaper didn't already have it. It loses some news value if the other paper ran it first or if it was on television first.

Morning newspapers especially like stories that break after the late evening news.

Many other elements aside from those mentioned come into play. They include progress, money, disaster, novelty, oddity, drama, children, animals, change, consequence, impact, rarity, coincidence. The list probably doesn't help much. Thoughtful examination of a good newspaper might. Most editors try for a blend of stories: Some local, some national, some international, something upbeat, something offbeat. A newspaper should be like a good meal, with lots of substance, balance—and a dash of dessert.

Practice and critical thinking develop news judgment. Perhaps the following exercises will help.

## Exercise 1

Here are 10 stories. You are an editor trying to decide which stories to put on the front page of your paper. You have room for five. Note the five stories you would select by letter, then explain the reasons for your selection.

a. A two-car collision kills two persons visiting from another state.
b. The City Council raises the city sales tax from one cent on the dollar to two cents on the dollar.
c. Congress passes a bill to add a wing to the main State Department building in Washington, D.C.
d. Rain finally ends a killer drought in Burkina Faso.
e. A professor studying all the towns in the country lists yours as the worst place to live.
f. The weather forecast says tomorrow will be just like today.
g. A new industry is coming to your town, bringing many new jobs.
h. An airplane crashes in Tokyo, killing 347 people, mostly Japanese.
i. A fire causes minor damage to the mayor's home while she is at a City Council meeting. No one is injured.
j. The attorney general of the United States is arrested and charged with littering after he is seen throwing an apple core out of a car window in Washington, D.C.

1. _____     2. _____     3. _____     4. _____     5. _____

COMMENTS:

_____

_____

_____

_____

_____

_____

_____

_____

_____

_____

_____

_____

_____

_____

_____

_____

_____

## Exercise 2

List the elements of news (if any) that would make these situations newsworthy.

a.  An Academy Award-winning actress sues her husband for divorce.

_____

_____

b.  200 people are held hostage by terrorists in Beirut.

_____

_____

c.  A whale swims the wrong way in a channel and is trapped. A nation is captivated by its struggle.

_____

_____

d.  Tomorrow is the first day of spring.

_____

_____

e.  An airplane crashes at a local airport.

_____

_____

f.  A former president of the United States dies.

_____

_____

g. A man bumps his head, recovers from amnesia, and returns to the wife he left 15 years earlier.

_____

_____

h. The local high school basketball team wins the state championship.

_____

_____

i. A lost cat returns home safely.

_____

_____

j. An airplane flies from Chicago to Des Moines.

_____

_____

k. The Republican National Convention opens.

_____

_____

l. A local woman celebrates her 92nd birthday.

_____

_____

m. A local man celebrates his 100th birthday.

_____

_____

n. A young woman from your town is named homecoming queen at State University 200 miles away.

_____

_____

o. Candidates for governor hold a debate.

_____

_____

p. A fight among players breaks out during a hockey game.

_____

_____

q. The mayor proclaims this week as Be Kind to Animals Week.

_____

_____

r. The City Council passes a resolution demanding that the federal government balance the budget.

_____

_____

s. Local high school journalism students win the Sweepstakes award in state competition.

_____

_____

t. A girl, 7, is enrolled in a high-school math class.

_____

_____

## Exercise 3

Below are the facts about an airplane accident. All the information came from the police. Write about the accident and be prepared to discuss the news judgment that affected your writing.

An airplane has crashed.

It crashed at 10:42 a.m. today.

No one was killed.

One person was injured.

The pilot walked away from the crash, unhurt.

A passenger suffered cuts and bruises.

The pilot is Vernon K. Armstrong, age 55.

He is from Walla Walla, Wash.

The passenger is Shirley A. Armstrong, 49, his wife.

She was rushed by ambulance to a nearby hospital.

Witnesses said the plane took off, rose 60 feet in the air and then crashed to the ground.

Mr. Armstrong is a veteran of the Vietnam War.

He won the Medal of Honor, the nation's highest military honor, for bravery during that war.

The plane was completely destroyed.

The plane was a small plane, a Cessna.

The crash occurred at Ourtown Municipal Airport.

The cause of the crash is unknown.

Mr. Armstrong told police he "just lost control."

_____

_____

_____

_____

_____

_____

_____

_____

_____

_____

_____

_____

## Exercise 4

To see how professional journalists use their judgment, study the front page of a local newspaper. Can you tell which story the editor considered the most important of the day? Is the main story local, national or international? Does the page have "dessert?" What impact did the time of the event covered have to do with where it was displayed? Write your comments below.

_____

_____

_____

_____

_____

_____

_____

_____

_____

_____

_____

_____

_____

# DOING
# INTERVIEWS

Successful reporters have many characteristics in common. They are all energetic, persistent, curious and knowledgeable, for example. They also are people who like people, and they know how to talk to others. In other words, they know how to conduct interviews—how to ask questions that get information from other people.

Good interviewing is a combination of many things. It involves planning—before the interview—to shape questions. Often, journalists have to ask questions without this planning, and the interview usually suffers because of it. Before interviews, journalists should think through what they're doing and decide what they want to find out. Then questions should be drawn up, with ice breakers at the beginning and more important questions at the middle or the end. A hazard here is that inexperienced journalists often rely too heavily on their lists and fail to ask follow-up questions. Journalists have to listen to the answers to their questions and frame new questions on the spot. This requires an alert mind—and practice. An appointment is required for most interviews if the reporter plans to take much of the source's time.

Some form of a note-taking system is essential. Formal shorthand or a speedwriting system that permits the reporter to write down key points verbatim while skeletonizing the rest can be used. The only requirement is that the reporter be able to read the notes when he or she gets ready to write the story. Many reporters use small tape recorders. Recorders permit the reporter to concentrate on the source and his or her words instead of on taking notes. But not all sources are comfortable when they are being taped, and this can put a crimp in the conversation. Even when using a recorder, the reporter should take notes on the most important points because it is difficult to locate a certain part of an interview, when you need it, on tape.

A straightforward, objective approach is the happy middle ground for most interviewers. This is better than trying to be coy or overly aggressive. The questions should be short and clear. Most of the time, open-ended, not yes-no, questions work best. The reporter should listen carefully and politely. If a question is not answered, the reporter should ask it again.

In ending an interview, the reporter should ask the source if he or she wants to add anything, just in case the questions didn't cover everything that needed covering. Also, the reporter probably should ask the source if it would be all right to contact him or her later if other questions come up.

**Exercise 1**

If you have an interview with the mayor of your city or town, what 10 questions would you ask?

_____

_____

_____

_____

_____

_____

_____

_____

_____

_____

_____

_____

_____

_____

_____

_____

## Exercise 2

If you have an interview with the editor of your local newspaper, what 10 questions would you ask the editor?

_____

_____

_____

_____

_____

_____

_____

_____

_____

_____

_____

_____

## Exercise 3

Below is a transcript of an interview. Comment and analyze the reporter's questions and technique.

Q. Could I have your exact name, please, and your age and address?
A. My name is Carole Hudson. I'm 50, and live at 610 S. Snyder St.

_____

_____

_____

Q. I understand you're planning to run for the state legislature, is that right?
A. Yes, that's why I asked you to come over to my office today.

_____

_____

_____

Q. You're a lawyer?
A. Yes. I'm a junior partner in the law firm of Ferguson and Patten.

_____

_____

_____


Q. A Republican, I'd guess.
A. No, I'm a Democrat.

_____

_____

_____


Q. Well, I didn't have time to study your record before coming over. Tell me more.
A. I was born in Lancaster, Pa., and I attended Franklin & Marshall College there before going to Harvard.

_____

_____

_____


Q. Your undergraduate degree is from Franklin & Marshall and your law degree is from Harvard, right?
A. That's correct.

_____

_____

_____


Q. Are you married?
A. Yes.

_____

_____

_____


Q. Uh, what's your husband's name, and what does he do?
A. His name is George, and he is a captain in the Ourtown Police Department.

_____

_____

_____

Q. Any kids?

A. Yes, we have one. Our daughter, Julie Ann, is working on a law degree at the University of Arizona.

_____

_____

_____

Q. How long have you lived here in Ourtown?

A. I moved here right after attending Harvard. Twenty-four years ago.

_____

_____

Q. Now, why do you want to be a state senator?

A. Well, I've been active in civic affairs, and I think I know my stuff about government, too. I am a life member of the Parent-Teacher Association and very concerned about schools. I was on the Ourtown Planning Commission, and I think our town is suffering from growth gone haywire. We must control this growth or we'll become just another city instead of the pleasant town we are now.

_____

_____

Q. Your opponent, the incumbent, Sen. Neal, has been in the legislature 12 years. He would be hard to beat.

A. Sure. It'll be tough. But I'm tough, too. I think I can beat him. I have put together a good organization, I've raised some money, and I think this town will rally for me. Sen. Neal has a very undistinguished record. I don't think he has ever sponsored a bill, and I know he has a lot of absenteeism. He misses more committee meetings than any other senator. He's very beatable, and I'm the person who can beat him.

_____

_____

Q. Well, I'm not so sure of that. But we'll see, won't we? What committees would you like to be on in the legislature if you get elected?

A. My first choice is education. I have a lot of interest there, as I told you. My second is agriculture. The farmers are hurting, and we need to help them.

_____

_____

_____

Q. Do you have a speciality as a lawyer?
A. I specialize in criminal law.

_____

_____

_____

Q. What kind of record did you have at Harvard?
A. I was editor of the Law Review and graduated second in my class.

_____

_____

_____

Q. You may have a fight just to win your party's nomination.
A. That's possible. We have a lot of good people in our party. But as the first to file, I
   think I'll have an advantage.

_____

_____

_____

Q. You have filed already?
A. Yes. I sent the papers to the Capital this morning.

_____

_____

_____

Q. Is there anything else you'd like to add? Anything I left out?
A. Not really. I'll just add that I am ready for this fight.

_____

_____

_____

Q. In case other questions come up later, would you mind if I contact you again?
A. No, not at all.

_____

_____

_____

Q. Thank you very much. I enjoyed talking with you.
A. Thank you. So did I.

_____

_____

## Exercise 4

Write a story based on the previous interview. Do you think you have all the information you need? What other questions should the reporter have asked?

_____

_____

_____

_____

_____

_____

_____

_____

_____

_____

_____

_____

_____

_____

_____

_____

_____

_____

_____

_____

# CHAPTER FOUR

# WRITING LEADS

In every classroom and newsroom in the land, journalists work hard to craft readable news stories. All of them agree: The first paragraph is the most important. If the first paragraph, or lead, doesn't hook the reader, then it is a flop. Readers have too many other things to do, and if the lead doesn't interest them, they will not read the story. They will mow the lawn or go shopping—or watch television.

Here are a few suggestions to keep in mind while working on leads. First, keep them short and to the point. The best leads usually are no more than two or three written lines, somewhere in the range of 12 to 17 words. (But don't sit around counting words!) Second, the lead should tell the reader what the story is about and recount the most essential news of the story. If the story is about a speech, the speaker's main points should be in the lead. If it's about a meeting, the main decisions made at the meeting should be in the lead. The rule is: Get to the point. Put the main facts in the lead.

Don't write:  The Student Council met Friday to elect new officers for next year.

Write:  Senior Patricia Apgar has been elected president of the Student Council for next year.

There are exceptions to these guidelines, of course. All stories are different, and certainly you would want to use different and novel approaches in feature writing or column writing. However, the vast majority of news stories are still constructed in the inverted pyramid style, the style in which important information is given at the top; being skillful in writing in that structure is crucial for any journalist.

Be careful not to clutter leads with nonessential information. In the story above, it is sufficient—in the lead—to announce the name of the new president. Somewhere in the story, of course, the day and place of the meeting, names of other new officers, etc. have a place. But not in the lead. The lead is a brief, concise summary of the most important fact (or facts) in the story. Most leads are one sentence long—but that's not an absolute. The rule is keep them short.

There was a time when journalists believed it necessary to get all the five *W's* and the *H* (who, what, where, when, why and how) in the lead. You don't see many such leads anymore. Today's lead is streamlined and to the point. Just remember that readers will not wait around for the news: it has to be in the lead—if it's straight news. The five *W's* and the *H* belong in almost all stories. But not in the first paragraph.

Leads that begin with a question—"Where is Ourtown headed this year?"—are usually unacceptable. Answer questions, don't ask them. Beginning a lead with a quote is also unacceptable—"I promise to do my best in my new office as Student Council president." You don't see many such leads in professional newspapers. That's the lazy person's way out.

The names of obscure organizations or associations do not belong in the lead. These names should be written after the lead paragraph.

Don't write:  The Department of Pharmacological Research at the Ferguson and Patten Institute for Environmental Studies today warned that the use of illegal drugs is harmful.

Write:  Use of illegal drugs is harmful, researchers warned today. Regular use of such drugs can cause dangerous side effects, according to a report from the Department of Pharmacological Research at the Ferguson and Patten Institute for Environmental Studies.

The following exercises will help you become familiar with writing this all-important paragraph.

## Exercise 1

Evaluate the following leads. What's wrong about these leads? What's right about them? If you object to a lead, suggest a better one.

a. Three seniors win scholarships.

_____

_____

_____

_____

b.  Ourtown High School's all-state center, James Donovan, has accepted a scholarship to play at State University, where he is expected to have a good chance to start as a freshman under Coach Walter Hughes' plan to let as many freshmen as he can see action early in their careers. We congratulate James.

_____

_____

_____

_____

c.  Principal William Howland announced this week that senior Sally Ann Mays will be appointed as his personal representative to a new Youth Council being formed by Ourtown Mayor Lois Wilcox.

_____

_____

_____

_____

d.  For the sixth year in a row, the marching band captures first place at the Harvest of Harmony Festival in Grand Island.

_____

_____

_____

_____

e.  ''Serving on the Student Council gives you a chance to serve the school in a very important way.''

_____

_____

_____

_____

f.  What happens to Ourtown High School's seniors after they graduate?

_____

_____

_____

_____

g.  22 Ourtown High School seniors have won college scholarships so far this year.

_____

_____

_____

_____

h.  Librarian Peggy Freeman said this week that 246 books are missing from Ourtown
High School libraries.

_____

_____

_____

_____

i.  A Students Against Drunk Driving (SADD) chapter has been formed at Ourtown High
School.

_____

_____

_____

_____

j.  Five new teachers joined the Ourtown High School faculty this year, bringing the total
number of teachers to 47.

_____

_____

_____

## Exercise 2

Try this type of exercise again. Here are 10 more leads. Which ones make you
want to read the rest of the story? Which ones do not? Why?

a.  With the scoreboard clock showing one second left and as 3,000 fans shrieked in unison,
senior Brad Levy stepped to the free-throw line.

_____

_____

_____

_____

b. Vandalism at Ourtown High School caused $13,000 in damages last year alone, and Principal Roger Malone said this week the problem ''must be solved.''

_____

_____

_____

_____

c. Students caught cheating on final exams will be expelled. Period.

_____

_____

_____

_____

d. At first she was shocked. Then she cried. Then, said new Homecoming Queen Lisa Green, ''I just got numb.''

_____

_____

_____

_____

e. On Friday, Sept. 24, at 9 a.m. in the morning, five new teachers will be presented at an assembly.

_____

_____

_____

_____

f. Summer brings heat, bathing suits, vacation.

_____

_____

_____

_____

g. In the spring, a young man's fancy turns to . . . baseball.

_____

_____

_____

h. With elections just around the corner, the staff of The Bugle conducted a poll to see which candidate the school favors.

_____

_____

_____

_____

i. We're No. 1!!

_____

_____

_____

_____

j. Planning begins soon for the first annual Mock United Nations event to be held this fall.

_____

_____

_____

## Exercise 3

Here are five poorly written leads. Rewrite each one to keep it short and to the point.

a. Prof. Michael Hosokawa of State University, an authority on Native American people and their social customs, will be the featured speaker at Ourtown High School's next assembly Friday, Oct. 21. The title of his speech will be "How We Can Help Preserve Native American Life."

_____

_____

_____

_____

_____

b.  Hey, out there. Someone isn't returning his library books. Students owe a total of $723 in fines for this year alone.

_____

_____

_____

_____

c.  The mighty Ourtown High School Golden Bears take on conference weak-sister Smithville this Friday. Make plans for your victory party now. The win will give OHS their third straight Dixie Conference title.

_____

_____

_____

_____

d.  Have you ever wondered what it would be like to stroll the streets of Tokyo and Hong Kong? Are you curious about the Orient and dying to see it? For senior Scott Campbell, the dream is about to come true. Scott has been selected to study for a year in Tokyo under a new program sponsored by the Ourtown Civic Club.

_____

_____

_____

_____

e.  "Live every day to its fullest. Learn something new each day. Enjoy life." That's the philosophy of Edward Ross, history teacher, who announced this week that he is retiring from Ourtown High School at the end of this year after 38 years on the faculty. He also believes, "Teaching here was the best decision I ever made. Leaving here is the hardest thing I've ever had to do."

_____

_____

_____

_____

## Exercise 4

Here is material for five stories. Write a lead for each one.

a. The Ourtown High School drama department is going to stage a play. The play will be performed Dec. 12 and Dec. 13 in the Main Auditorium at 7:30 p.m. The play will be "Sweeney Todd: The Demon Barber of Fleet Street." Brent Snow, a senior, has been chosen for the title role. The audience will be encouraged to participate by booing and hissing at the performers. Rehearsal starts Monday, Oct. 12. Both drama classes will help stage the show. Sponsor and director of the play will be Helen Mays, head of the drama department.

_____

_____

_____

_____

b. Enrollment at Outown High School is up this year from last year. Last year, the school had 457 students. This year, enrollment is 502. That's an increase of 45 students. Most of the increase seems to be in the freshman class, Principal Robert Slote said. He added that he was "delighted" by the increase. "The more the merrier," he said. He also said the school's budget goes up with its enrollment. "We can always use more money," he said.

_____

_____

_____

_____

c. An Ourtown High School student has been selected as a finalist in a national contest to design a poster for the Drunk Driving Awareness Campaign. His name is Jim Bishop and he is a senior. Asked about his reactions to being chosen, Bishop said, "I am thrilled, delighted, happy. This is a real honor for me and the school." His poster previously had been declared the regional winner. The national first place winner will get a $1,000 scholarship for college.

_____

_____

_____

_____

d. Journalism adviser Phyllis Megay and 10 students from the Ourtown High School Bugle attended a conference at State University on Nov. 4–5 sponsored by the journalism department of State University. Total attendance was 300. Journalists and journalism professors from all over the state also attended. Results of the yearly contest for high school journalists were announced. The Bugle was declared the best newspaper in the state for the third straight year. Ms. Megay said of the award, "I could get used to this."

_____

_____

_____

_____

_____

e. Ourtown Principal Robert Slote announced a new plan last Monday, Oct. 3. He said a special telephone number was now available to all algebra and geometry students. He called it his "Dial a Teacher Program." With this number, 555-8513, students will be able to reach a teacher who can help with a homework problem. The line will be answered Tuesdays, Wednesdays and Thursdays from 5 p.m. to 8 p.m. Slote encouraged all math students to use the line "as often as necessary."

_____

_____

_____

_____

## Exercise 5

Here is material for five more stories. Write a creative, feature-type lead for each one.

a. Freshman Bernice Walsh has a pet boa constrictor. It is six feet long and six months old. She keeps it at home. It has a cage to sleep in but usually "has the run of the house," she said. She says, "I'm not afraid of any old snake." The snake's name is Bubbles. It was a birthday present from her older sister, Jan, who is a biologist at State University. Bernice says her parents didn't want her to have the snake but that her sister convinced them it would not harm anyone. When Bubbles is a year old, the family plans to donate it to the City Zoo. Bernice says she doesn't know if Bubbles is a boy or girl.

_____

_____

_____

b. Ourtown High School has a 10-year-old student. Her name is Lisa Talese. She is a freshman. She has an IQ of 190. The school district urged her parents to place her several years ahead of her classmates because they were afraid she would be bored with elementary school work. Lisa plays four musical instruments, beats her home computer regularly in chess, and already has been invited to apply to three Ivy League schools. She is taking history, geometry, English, French and chorus. She has never missed a day of school and never received a grade below an A. Both of her parents teach at State University. She says she likes OHS ''a lot.'' ''The kids are all nice to me. At first they looked at me kind of funny. But now they accept me.'' She is 4 feet 9 inches tall and weighs 85 pounds.

_____

_____

_____

_____

c. Two Ourtown High School seniors are claiming a world record. They have asked that the *Guinness Book of World Records* include their names in the next edition. They played chess for 36 straight hours, pausing only long enough for quick meals and, once, a shower. The two are Dale Whittaker and Bill Moore. They are both members of the OHS Chess Club. They played at Dale's house. They played 22 games. Each won 10 and two were stalemates. When their marathon was over, they each slept for 10 hours. Both said they dreamed of chess.

_____

_____

_____

_____

d. A stray dog visited Ourtown High School last Friday, Oct. 22. No one knows where the dog came from. It first was seen in the journalism lab. When students called it, it ran down the hall and into an empty chemistry lab. It upset some test tubes, spilling several experiments. From there, it trotted into a speech class, interrupting a mock debate on animal rights. Then it left. It was last seen going out the east doors.

_____

_____

_____

_____

e. The senior class has a new project. The class is asking all members to collect aluminium cans and to turn them in for recycling. The class hopes to raise $150 to help with the annual senior trip. Class members are asked to get their families involved in the project. The drive will go on all month, according to history teacher Carol Blythe, class sponsor.

_____

_____

_____

# CHAPTER FIVE

# WRITING NEWS STORIES

Writing the lead is half the battle. Writing the rest of the story is the other half.

As mentioned before, most news stories are written in inverted pyramid form, which means that the main facts are written first, and the secondary facts are written in descending order of importance. Imagine an upside-down pyramid. The broadest part of the pyramid is the lead, and as the facts become less important, the pyramid narrows. This form of newswriting allows the reader to get the most important information in the first paragraph. And if the story needs to be shortened, it can be lopped off from the bottom with little damage.

The problem with inverted pyramid form is deciding which fact is more important than the other. Arranging the facts, or paragraphs, together to complete the story, is a greater skill. The paragraphs cannot merely be piled on top of each other. They have to relate. They need transitions to bring them together. To emphasize the importance of transitions and of placing related facts together, think of a spiral-shaped pyramid, or of a tornado.

Paragraphs in news stories should be kept short, about three or four lines. This is to keep the newspaper from looking gray when the words are squeezed into narrow columns. Most of the paragraph rules followed in English class are invalid in journalism class. Newspaper paragraphs are almost exclusively typographical, not literary, devices.

When writing the news story, always tell readers where the information came from. This is called attribution. Readers have to know the origin of the facts so as to judge their value or truth.

Keep in mind that you must remain objective. The news story is no place for the writer's own feelings. Opinions can be expressed in editorials or columns, and, to some small extent, in feature stories. But not in news stories.

Good quotations make news stories more readable. Many people believe the best quote of the story should come in the second paragraph. This is called a backup quote, because it "backs up," or elaborates on, the lead.

Avoid cliches (busy as bees, hard as nails). The rule is, if the writer has seen the figure of speech in print many times before, he or she should not use it. However, there is no rule against inventing new figures of speech.

In addition to avoiding cliches, you also should avoid using jargons, the inside language of groups. Police officers may say they are looking for "three parties in a vehicle," but journalists must write that police officers are looking for "three people in a car." Journalists have their own jargon, of course. For example, the newspaper library is referred to as a "morgue." But journalists should never use this jargon in a news story. They use plain, simple, straightforward language. They want to convey facts, not display their vocabularies. The goal is clarity. Use short words, short sentences and short paragraphs.

Newswriting is bare, lean, precise and concise. All extra words must be edited out. Look at the difference between the following sentences.

Don't write: Due to the fact that it was Easter Sunday, all of the stores were closed.

Write: Because it was Easter, all the stores were closed.

Avoid redundancy. For example, "He was a Jewish rabbi." All rabbis are Jewish. Do not write "The accident occurred at the intersection of First and Main streets." First and Main *is* an intersection. Make every word count. Take out every word that doesn't.

Look closely at all adjectives and adverbs. Most of the time they drain the effectiveness of the writing rather than enhance it.

Stay away from euphemisms. If someone dies, the word to use is "died," not "passed away" or "joined the great silent majority in the sky." Say what you mean.

Use concrete language not abstract language. Do not say someone is short. Say he is 5 feet 2 inches tall and let the reader decide. "Short" means one thing to a jockey and something else to the National Basketball Association.

Make sure all of your facts are accurate and each word spelled correctly. Accuracy is absolutely essential. There is no place in journalism for writers who cannot get their facts straight. Check. Double check. Read the copy again for accuracy and spelling. The old saying is, "You say your mother loves you? Check it out!"

The following exercises will help sharpen your accuracy, editing and writing skills.

## Exercise 1

Below are 20 of the most commonly misspelled words. Some are spelled correctly, others are not. Using copy-editing symbols (see Appendix B), correct the misspelled words.

| | | | |
|---|---|---|---|
| cemetary | hemorrhage | defendant | ammendment |
| sheriff | harrass | alright | liason |
| accomodate | receive | Anartic | satellite |
| superintendant | commitee | Connecticut | Mississippi |
| sargeant | amount | nuclear | permissable |

## Exercise 2

Here are 20 more of the most commonly misspelled words. Using copy-editing symbols, correct the misspelled words.

| | | | |
|---|---|---|---|
| underway | forcast | percieve | alot |
| penitentiary | consensus | pardner | misspell |
| embarras | occured | municiple | conscience |
| sucess | develop | neccessary | connoisseur |
| principle (of the school) | seperate | better (one who bets) | affidavid |

## Exercise 3

Below are 20 pairs of words. Circle the word that is spelled correctly in each pair.

| | | | |
|---|---|---|---|
| cellar | celler | flourescent | fluorescent |
| souvenair | souvenir | extention | extension |
| questionnaire | questionaire | missle | missile |
| forty | fourty | assisstant | assistant |
| suppress | supress | ecstasy | ectacy |
| resind | rescind | definitely | definately |
| carburetor | carburator | computor | computer |
| resuscitate | resusitate | sieze | seize |
| buoy | bouy | yeild | yield |
| Cincinnati | Cincinatti | paralel | parallel |

## Exercise 4

Here are 20 more pairs of words. Circle the word that is spelled correctly in each pair.

| | | | |
|---|---|---|---|
| villian | villain | barbecue | barbeque |
| dilema | dilemma | grammer | grammar |
| psychiatrist | pyschiatrist | Albuquerque | Albuquerkue |
| sophmore | sophomore | concensus | consensus |
| dormitory | dormitery | silouette | silhouette |
| insistent | insistant | imposter | impostor |
| vacuum | vaccuum | calender | calendar |
| achieve | acheive | paraphenalia | paraphernalia |
| paid | payed | privilege | privilidge |
| occassionally | occasionally | decieve | deceive |

## Exercise 5

To further sharpen your spelling skills, here are 20 more pairs of words. Circle the word which is spelled correctly in each pair.

| | | | |
|---|---|---|---|
| guerilla | guerrilla | excell | excel |
| catagory | category | accordion | accordian |
| fiery | firey | restaurant | restarant |
| ninty | ninety | supprise | surprise |
| argument | arguement | culinary | cullinary |
| Carribbean | Caribbean | dependant | dependent |
| marjuana | marijuana | collission | collision |
| homocide | homicide | counterfit | counterfeit |
| chauffeur | chaufer | wintery | wintry |
| accellerate | accelerate | conscience | concience |

## Exercise 6

Newswriting is bare, lean, precise and concise. Find a shorter or simpler word for each of the following.

| | | | |
|---|---|---|---|
| ponder | _____ | inundate | _____ |
| affluent | _____ | opulent | _____ |
| municipal | _____ | utilize | _____ |
| instruct | _____ | infrequent | _____ |
| remedy | _____ | powerful | _____ |
| deceased | _____ | allude | _____ |
| attempt | _____ | lacerations | _____ |
| contusions | _____ | purchase | _____ |
| conceal | _____ | witness | _____ |
| possess | _____ | solitary | _____ |

## Exercise 7

The following terms can be replaced with shorter or simpler words. Find a better word for each one.

| | | | |
|---|---|---|---|
| verbalize | _____ | address | _____ |
| interrogate | _____ | commence | _____ |
| reside | _____ | terminate | _____ |
| assist | _____ | felines | _____ |
| residence | _____ | intoxicated | _____ |
| disadvantaged | _____ | improper | _____ |
| purloin | _____ | community | _____ |
| configuration | _____ | gratuity | _____ |
| genuine | _____ | exhibit | _____ |
| recuperate | _____ | remainder | _____ |
| approximately | _____ | encounter | _____ |

## Exercise 8

Again, the following words can be simplified or shortened. Think of a better word for each one and write it down.

Answers may vary.

| | | | |
|---|---|---|---|
| concept | _____ | incarcerate | _____ |
| impoverished | _____ | antiquated | _____ |
| implement | _____ | employment | _____ |
| conflagration | _____ | fatigued | _____ |
| ambiguous | _____ | interment | _____ |
| illumination | _____ | inevitable | _____ |
| terminate | _____ | improbable | _____ |
| numerous | _____ | penitent | _____ |
| selection | _____ | incorrect | _____ |
| indolent | _____ | sorrowfully | _____ |

## Exercise 9

Edit the following sentences to remove all unnecessary words. You may need to rewrite some of the sentences.

a. The principal announced that she had tendered her resignation.

_____

b. The committee gave its approval.

_____

c. The attack took place at 12 noon.

_____

d. The troops were surrounded on all sides.

_____

e. The globe is spherical in shape.

_____

f. She is of the opinion that man will reach Mars in the near future.

_____

g. He called a press conference to announce his future plans.

_____

h. At that time, no one understood the problem.

_____

i. He was taken into custody and placed in jail.

_____

j. The bouquet of flowers cost him the sum of $40.

_____

k. Police announced that a dead body had been found.

_____

l. Income for the month of May set a new record.

_____

m. Students in the city of Chicago were engaged in studying.

_____

n. She is currently starring on Broadway but will return back home soon.

_____

o. Police made an investigation but have no comment to make at the present time.

_____

p. The speaker told his listeners his wife had given birth to a baby boy.

_____

q. The committee held a meeting Friday and made an announcement that its advance predictions were correct.

_____

r. Police determined that the victim had been strangled to death.

_____

s. The meeting will be held for the purpose of discussing other alternatives.

_____

t. In the event that she talks on the subject of journalism during the course of the day, students should be ready and prepared to take notes.

_____

## Exercise 10

To make the following sentences more concise, edit or rewrite each one to remove all unnecessary words.

a. It was the consensus of opinion that it was an old antique.

_____

b. The committee held a meeting for the purpose of checking plans for the summer months.

_____

c. An assembled crowd of people gathered in the city of Shreveport.

_____

d. She made the presentation at the hour of noon.

_____

e. He decided to make a journey to the Capitol to give a performance.

_____

f. Citizens filed a complaint, demanding a definite commitment.

_____

g.  Some residents protested against the plan.

_____

k.  Students were asked to refer back to past history.

_____

l.  For a period of two weeks in 1986, the present incumbent had an office at the corner of 9th and Hoover streets.

_____

m.  The crash completely destroyed the airplane.

_____

n.  Two people from Texas were united in holy matrimony.

_____

o.  Due to the fact that writing skills are important, the school will hold a writing clinic during the month of September.

_____

p.  The meeting will be held beginning at 10 a.m. in the morning.

_____

q.  When the game finally ended, the crowd cheered.

_____

r.  The hotel noted that we had not made advance reservations.

_____

s.  Police were looking for a red-colored car.

_____

t.  Students are asked to bring textbooks with them.

_____

## Exercise 11

The following are filled with cliches, trite expressions and worn-out figures of speech. Edit or rewrite each sentence to remove the overused expressions.

a. She entered the ballroom looking as fresh as a daisy.

_____

b. When the dust finally settled, Ourtown had won, 3–2.

_____

c. When the smoke cleared, the measure passed unanimously.

_____

d. Police arrived just in the nick of time.

_____

e. After a whirlwind visit, the candidate expected the lion's share of the votes.

_____

f. He said his campaign offered a two-pronged approach, but said neither was set in stone.

_____

g. The bottom line in this case is financing.

_____

h. At this point in time, we cannot afford this project.

_____

i. The ships limped into port.

_____

j. She asked the driver to hang a left.

_____

k.  They were between a rock and a hard place.

l.  The Super Bowl always generates media hype.

m.  The offense functioned like a well-oiled machine but it was the D that won the game.

n.  He threw the ball straight as an arrow.

o.  This is only the tip of the iceberg of this problem.

p.  He fired off a letter leveling the attack.

q.  A rule of thumb is to avoid cliches like the plague.

r.  Consumers, already used to tightening their belts, were asked this week to bite the bullet.

s.  We won't beat around the bush: This exercise is your acid test.

t.  Lady Luck smiled on the Wildcats for a time last night—but that was the calm before the storm.

## Exercise 12

Journalists must remain objective. Some of the sentences below contain words or phrases of judgment and opinion. Edit or rewrite the sentences to eliminate these judgment of opinions.

a. The Drama Club on Friday will present a dazzling performance of the exciting hit Broadway musical "Annie."

_____

_____

_____

b. Displaying a charming smile and wearing chic golden earrings, Homecoming Queen Anna Forrester strode to her flower-covered throne.

_____

_____

_____

c. A narrow 2–1 victory permitted the Golden Bears to compete in the regional baseball finals in a district widely regarded as the toughest in the state.

_____

_____

_____

d. The principal told us that unless we improve our grades, we will be ranked behind some of the school's biggest academic rivals.

_____

_____

_____

_____

e. Our Golden Bears are on the road Friday, seeking their fifth straight victory over conference weak sister Stateville.

_____

_____

_____

f. It's going to be hot tomorrow, with temperatures reaching a blazing 92 degrees.

_____

_____

_____

g. The Student Council on Monday made a great decision when it decided to urge teachers not to give tests on the last day of class.

_____

_____

_____

h. Congress passed a bill Friday aimed at stopping runaway inflation and easing the problems of jobless Americans.

_____

_____

_____

i. Strong winds of 60 miles an hour buffeted California's rocky, fog-covered shoreline, sending shivering surfers to look for a warm place.

_____

_____

_____

j. We have the best school in the state because our SAT scores led all other schools.

_____

_____

_____

# Exercise 13

Each of the sentences below contains an error. Find the error in each one to correct the sentence.

a. This test will have an affect on your grade.

_____

_____

b. The red-headed senior guard scored the winning basket.

_____

_____

c. The school will be closed for the foreseeable future.

_____

_____

d. Many refugees are dyeing of hunger and disease.

_____

_____

e. Funeral services will be Sunday.

_____

_____

f. The game was cancelled due to the weather.

_____

_____

g. The city will host next year's convention.

_____

_____

h. You will all do alright on this quiz.

_____

_____

i. Afterwards, they decided to visit the city.

_____

_____

j. Journalism operates on lofty principals.

_____

_____

k. We are in a very unique situation.

_____

_____

l. Members balloted on the new officers.

_____

_____

m. The suspect alluded police.

_____

_____

n. The council voted a hike in taxes.

_____

_____

o. The coach was pleased by the team's assent in the rankings.

_____

_____

p. The bald-headed man surrendered to police.

_____

_____

q. The instructor was pleased by the complement.

_____

_____

r. The suspect said he was entitled to council.

_____

_____


s. The City Council passed the ordnance.

_____

_____


t. She said she didn't know whether to go or not.

_____

_____


## Exercise 14

Think of transitions as turn signals, little signs that readers follow as they move from idea to idea. Each of the paragraphs below contains transitional devices, such as repetition of a key word or use of the word *also,* that link one sentence or paragraph to another. Circle the word(s) used as transitions in the following news story.

The Ourtown Board of Education on Monday accepted the resignation of OHS Principal Arthur Goodguy. The board said in a statement that it accepted the resignation ''with regret.''

''I regret it, too,'' Goodguy said. ''I really like it here.'' Goodguy told the board he was resigning to enroll in a doctoral program in school administration at State University. The board passed a resolution praising Goodguy for his work in the two years he has served.

In other action, the board tabled a plan to examine the school's academic policies as they relate to athletic participation. The plan had been submitted by Superintendent Aleesa Allison. Early today, Allison said she was ''terribly disappointed'' by the action.

''I really thought it was a good plan,'' she said. ''I thought it had merit. But that's not the first time I've been disappointed.''

On another matter, the board approved a 5 percent increase in the OHS budget for the next fiscal year. However, Board President Henry Archer said the increase would be ''eaten up by inflation.'' ''Inflation is the real enemy of our school programs,'' he added.

Another school enemy, littering, was considered in a report submitted by the OHS Student Council. The council called for stiffer penalties to be imposed upon students caught littering. The board thanked the students but took no action.

## Exercise 15

With the help of your classmates and teacher, create a local style sheet for use in your school publications. For example, the style sheet should list if your school name is referred to as Ourtown High School or OHS in first reference. Should the school nickname precede the sports team's name in news stories? Is it sufficient to write OLB in first reference for Old Library Building? Your local style sheet can be as short as a page or as long as three pages.

_____

_____

_____

_____

_____

_____

_____

_____

_____

_____

_____

_____

_____

_____

_____

_____

_____

_____

_____

_____

_____

_____

_____

_____

## Exercise 16

Write a news story using the following information. If attribution is needed, use Mrs. Franklin as the source.

She said she was "very, very surprised" by the award because she did not know she had been nominated.

Last year, students voted Mrs. Franklin "Teacher of the Year." She was presented a bouquet of flowers at the Senior Assembly last year.

This year's physics award carries a one-thousand-dollar cash prize.

Mrs. Franklin said her favorite color is blue and her favorite TV show is the "Bill Cosby Show."

The award is called an Award for Excellence in Physics Teaching.

It is given by the American Association of Physics Teachers.

Mrs. Franklin said she learned of the award from a phone call.

The caller was Prof. Jonathan Ronin of State University.

He was her physics teacher when she was in college.

He nominated her for the award.

Mrs. Vera Franklin teaches physics at Ourtown High School.

She has been on the faculty for 10 years.

She is a graduate of State University.

She was selected as one of five physics teachers in the state to win an award.

_____

_____

_____

_____

_____

_____

_____

_____

_____

_____

_____

_____

_____

_____

_____

_____

_____

_____

## Exercise 17

Write a story using the following information. If attribution is needed, your source is Student Council Homecoming Chairwoman Melissa Clark.

The dance will be Saturday at City Auditorium from 8 p.m. in the evening to 12 midnight.

A bonfire at City Park will be held Thursday, Oct. 10.

The fire begins at 8.

The bonfire will be sponsored by the Student Council.

Students attending the bonfire are asked to contribute one dollar to the Student Council's scholarship fund.

The King and Queen will be crowned at halftime of Friday's game.

Next weekend is Homecoming for Ourtown High School.

The date is Friday, Oct. 11, and Saturday, Oct. 12.

Friday's game at 7:30 p.m. is between OHS and Smithville.

OHS can win the Dixie Conference championship with a win.

Elections for homecoming king and queen begin Monday, Oct. 8.

The king candidates, all seniors, are Bill Lee, David Shapiro and Luis Ramirez. The queen candidates, all seniors, are Lisa Green, Ellen Loo and Kim Murphy.

## Exercise 18

Develop a news story from the following information provided. If attribution is needed, use History Instructor Donald Merritt as your source.

Said Mr. Merritt: ''We don't have a very big problem in our school yet. But we know we can't avoid it forever, and we want to be ready.''

It has twenty-two members.

The adviser for this group is History Instructor Donald Merritt.

The group meets Fridays during lunch period.

The group was formed to promote awareness of drug and alcohol problems.

Students with questions or concerns about drugs or alcohol are welcome to attend.

The group's president is Shawn McFarland, a senior.

The vice president is Kim Hendrix, a junior.

The secretary-treasurer is Jason Krauss, a sophomore.

A new student group has been formed at Ourtown High School.

The group is called the Student Support Group.

_____

_____

_____

_____

_____

_____

_____

_____

_____

_____

_____

_____

# Exercise 19

Write a news story from the information below, gathered at a meeting of the Board of Education.

The Board of Education met Monday, May 1.

All members were present.

President Leonard Hammond presided.

The meeting began at 7 p.m.

Approximately 152 persons attended.

The minutes of the last meeting were read and approved.

The board heard a report from Superintendent Arlene P. Dunlap that enrollment in the district is up 18 percent from last year.

Dunlap called this "disturbing because we are running out of space in our classrooms, and education is suffering because of it."

She asked the board to approve a $3.3 million building program for the district.

The money would build two new elementary schools and a new junior high school.

The board voted 4–2 to place the issue as a referendum on the November general election ballot.

Voting for placing the referendum on the ballot were Hammond, George Bailey, Ellen Massey and Ramon Chavez.

Voting against placing the referendum on the ballot were Jack Armstrong and Verne Shestak.

Armstrong shouted, "This is a waste of the taxpayer's money!"

Hammond observed, "You are out of order, Mr. Armstrong."

A member of the audience muttered, "Let him speak."

Ms. Massey said, "Clearly, quite clearly, we need these new schools. We are 50 years behind the times in this town."

One of the new elementary schools would be built on the east side of town, the other on the west. The junior high school would be built in the central part of town.

The meeting adjourned at 9:37 p.m.

Asked to comment on the referendum issue, Senior Class President Kimberly Hawkins said, "Sounds good to me."

_____

_____

_____

_____

_____

_____

_____

_____

_____

_____

_____

_____

_____

_____

_____

_____

_____

_____

_____

_____

_____

_____

_____

_____

_____

_____

_____

_____

_____

_____

_____

_____

_____

_____

_____

_____

_____

_____

## Exercise 20

To further sharpen your newswriting skills, write a news story from the information below. Unless otherwise noted, use Journalism Adviser Phyllis Megay as your source.

The Ourtown High School Bugle has been named the best scholastic newspaper in the state for the third straight year.

This occurred at a conference at State University Nov. 4–5.

10 journalism students and Ms. Megay attended.

Journalism professors and professional journalists from around the state attended.

300 people in all attended.

Bugle Editor-in-chief Kelly Wiese exclaimed, ''We knew we could do it again. We have a great teacher and the best journalism program in America!''

Various contests were conducted in conjunction with the convention.

Kelly was named first-place winner over all other entrants in editorial writing.

Sports Editor Kirk Wilson won first in sports column writing.

Photographer Liz Englehardt took second for a feature photo.

The Bugle was judged second-best in the competition for first-page design and layout.

Megay is a former staff member of the Des Moines (Iowa) Register. She holds a journalism degree from Iowa State University.

_____

_____

_____

_____

_____

_____

_____

_____

_____

_____

_____

_____

_____

_____

_____

_____

_____

# USING QUOTES

Journalists do many types of stories: Eyewitness accounts, interpretive stories requiring great expertise, features about people and holidays. The list is endless. Many stories are simple accounts of what people tell journalists. For example, to find out about the progress on the construction of a new school, the reporter asks the person who is overseeing the project. Then the reporter quotes that person. How do journalists handle quotes? This chapter will help answer this question.

Many issues are involved. But none is greater than accuracy. Quotes must be exact. Quotation marks placed around a word, a phrase or a sentence signal to the reader that these are the sources's exact words. Most journalists feel it is fair to make small adjustments in a quote if the source makes a grammatical error or uses profanity. But these are exceptions. The rule is: Quotation marks mean these are the source's exact words. To the journalist, this means listening carefully and taking good notes.

It doesn't mean, however, that you *have* to use the source's exact words in all cases. You can use your words and the source's ideas. This is called paraphrasing, and it works like this.

Don't write:  "We have 5,672 volumes in the library, and our budget for next year is $76,542," the librarian said.

Write:  He said the library has 5,672 books and a budget next year of $76,542.

You do not use quotation marks when paraphrasing. Although the sentences represent the source's ideas, the words are yours.

Paraphrasing also can make a story more concise, eliminate long and windy passages, and sometimes can simplify technical language.

Another advantage in using quotes is that they help make a story colorful and bright. The sound of human voices belongs in most stories. Readers can understand people better if they can see their exact words. So make direct quotes out of the best material the source utters. But don't use quotes to convey facts. In the example above, the source is merely conveying facts and there is no reason to use his words. If the librarian previously quoted added, "And if we don't get a new building, I'm going to burn this old one down," then you would make this into a direct quote. The rule is: Make direct quotes out of colorful, dramatic or interesting material. Use your own words to convey facts.

Don't write: "The play begins at 7:30 p.m., and the tickets $1.50," she said.

Write: The play begins at 7:30 p.m. Tickets are $1.50.

You may use, ethically, what are called partial quotes. Let us say, you are interviewing a source and she utters a sentence that contains a phrase you like. It is all right to use just that phrase in your story. If the source said, "So, at the end of the school year, after 35 years on the faculty, I am going to shuffle out of this place for a well-earned rest," you can write: She said she would retire at the end of the year and "shuffle out of this place." Be careful not to overuse partial quotes, however. They might create distortion or choppiness in the copy. Here is an example:

> Police said they were "stunned and angry" after an "angry, howling mob" began throwing rocks. Police were "doing their duty," the mayor said, describing the protestors as "chilling" to negotiations. A protester said he was "clubbed twice" by officers, and said they called him a "no-good thug."

All these little bits and pieces of sentences are distracting to the reader.

When sources are quoted, journalists must decide what verb to use in attributing or sourcing of the quote. There are three schools of thought on attribution. One says journalists should always use "said." Another says journalists should not repeat "said" more than a couple of times in any one story and should use other verbs of attribution, such as "added," or "noted" or "stated." The third school of thought is in the middle, and this is what we endorse. Use "said" most of the time, for it has no editorial overtones. It doesn't suggest anything except that these words were uttered by that person. Many verbs of attribution have hooks to them—that is they imply or suggest something. For example, "charged" and "claimed" are loaded words. "Commented" suggests something not very important and "added" implies the quote is an afterthought.

This doesn't mean journalists should use "said" in every instance. If it's a question—"Where are you going?" she asked—then obviously "asked" is all right. The advice is: Use "said" most of the time but take the good opportunities that present themselves to use another verb.

Make sure the verb of attribution does not represent impossibilities. "I hate this course," he shrugged. You cannot shrug words. "It's not my problem," she smiled. You cannot smile words. Or cough them, or sigh them or breathe them.

The following exercises will help you understand the issue of attribution of quotes in journalism.

## Exercise 1

Here is a list of verbs used in attribution or sourcing of quotations. Write N if the verb is neutral or objective and X if it is not. Briefly explain your choice in the space provided, noting when it is appropriate to use that word or words and any connotations that word may have.

say _____

add _____

charge _____

shout _____

shoot back _____

demand _____

bellow _____

conclude _____

allege _____

note _____

report _____

answer _____

state _____

retort _____

preach _____

roar _____

comment _____

assert _____

muse _____

declare _____

## Exercise 2

Below is a series of direct quotes. Paraphrase each one.

a. ''And so, at the conclusion of this long campaign, this long and rugged campaign that began so many months ago, I want to make one thing perfectly clear. No American will ever have to be without a job as long as I am in the White House. Nor will we become involved in a military conflict. And as a final vow, my fellow Americans, just let me say that my administration will be as clean as a hound's tooth.''

_____

_____

_____

_____

b. ''So I say without fear of contradiction—how could anyone contradict a team that is 12-0—that the Texas Longhorns are America's finest college football team, and I think the final polls will show us atop the standings again. Hook 'em Horns!''

_____

_____

_____

_____

c. ''Therefore, we on the selection committee to pick a new principal for Ourtown High School do wholeheartedly and with sincere enthusiasm, propose to this group that the school hire Mr. William R. Samoy as its new principal. He is a fine man, a Harvard graduate and one of America's distinguished educators. He is the right man for this difficult job, believe me.''

_____

_____

_____

_____

d. ''It is a fact of American life that we have many, many disadvantaged people, people whose lifestyles are dictated to them by their economic deprivation. We estimate the number of such unfortunate people at 25,000 in this state alone.''

_____

_____

_____

_____

e. "We were flying at about 3,000 feet, or maybe it was 4,000. I don't remember for sure. I heard a sound like a thud in the engine. The copilot reached for the controls. He's lefthanded, you know, and he took over. I went back to check on the passengers. They all seemed all right. I went back to the cockpit and discovered smoke coming out of the engine, smoke like thick oil smoke. The kind you see coming out of refineries. By then we were getting landing instructions. We put the plane down at Midway Airport. Nobody got hurt, thank God."

_____

_____

_____

_____

## Exercise 3

Read the story below and carefully look at how attribution is handled. Note your reaction to each quote below. If you feel the attribution is inappropriate, suggest a better verb or method of handling the quote.

[1]Ourtown Police Department is understaffed and underfinanced, Chief Clifton L. Ryan charged today.

[2]"When is this city going to wake up?" he growled to reporters at a press conference at City Hall.

[3]"We have 43 uniformed officers working in three divisions trying to cover a town of 51.3 square miles. Our budget rose 3.3 percent this year and we are expecting a 4.2 percent increase next year. That is simply not enough to do the job," he said.

[4]"Ourtown is growing very rapidly," he noted, adding that "growth is this city's worst problem."

[5]Asked how long he had been concerned about staffing and financing of the department, Ryan replied, "As long as I've been in this job."

[6]Records indicate he has been police chief for six years.

[7]Ryan demanded that the City Council approve 17 new officers, and he alleged that the department needs a 26 percent increase next year.

[8]"My hands are tied by this budget," he commented. "We can't do the job without tools," he added.

[9]He promised to try to "do my best" even if the new officers and increased budget are not approved.

[10]"But I won't like it," he grimaced.

1. _____

_____

_____

2. _____

_____

_____

3. _____

_____

_____

4. _____

_____

_____

5. _____

_____

_____

6. _____

_____

_____

7. _____

_____

_____

8. _____

_____

_____

9. _____

_____

_____

10. _____

_____

_____

## Exercise 4

Evaluate the use of quotation marks and methods of attribution in the following sentences. Each sentence needs editing.

a. She said the course was ''Mickey Mouse.''

_____

_____

_____

b.  Sally was described as a "snob" by her friends.

_____

_____

_____

_____

c.  The hospital spokesman said her condition was "critical."

_____

_____

_____

_____

d.  Police described the suspect as "armed and dangerous."

_____

_____

_____

_____

e.  The office said it expected an "increase" in sales.

_____

_____

_____

_____

f.  "The man is a louse," she explained.

_____

_____

_____

_____

g.  "The governor is a crook," he noted.

_____

_____

_____

_____

h. She feels left out of the activities.

_____

_____

_____

_____

i. Asked what it felt like at the moment of liftoff, he said, "It was the most exciting moment of my life!"

_____

_____

_____

_____

j. "I got an A on the history exam," he confessed.

_____

_____

_____

_____

## Exercise 5

Again, the quotes and attribution in the sentences below are handled incorrectly. Explain what is wrong with each sentence, rewriting as necessary.

a. The professor was upset. "It is too early to be lecturing."

_____

_____

_____

_____

b. "You bother me," she coughed.

_____

_____

_____

_____

c. "Let me introduce myself," he concluded.

_____

_____

_____

_____

d. He said the music "thrilled" him.

_____

_____

_____

_____

e. "What time is it now?" he said.

_____

_____

_____

_____

f. "I love this game," the coach said. "It is great to be here," he added. "I hope I never have to leave," he continued.

_____

_____

_____

_____

g. "So I have decided not to run for re-election," he concluded. He added, "But I might change my mind."

_____

_____

_____

_____

h. "There is no way we can lose the game," the quarterback pointed out.

_____

_____

_____

_____

i. "The pitch I hit for the winning run was low and outside. But—Pow!—I gave it a shot and out it went—into the seats," he stated.

_____

_____

_____

_____

j. She hopes she will be our country's first woman president.

_____

_____

_____

## Exercise 6

Read each paragraph in the story below and explain if the attribution has been handled well. If you feel the attribution is inappropriate, write how it can be improved.

[1]Mayor Good Guy announced Friday he would seek re-election next year.

[2]"I have decided to go for it," he said, adding:

[3]"I have given good government to this city for three years. I feel the people want me to remain in office."

[4]He asserted again that his administration was free of corruption despite charges from his opponents that he was taking kickbacks on city contracts.

[5]"Those charges are bunk," Guy said. "I have never, repeat never, taken any kickbacks."

[6]But he noted that in response to the charges, he has begun an investigation. He promised to "get to the bottom of this business once and for all."

[7]Guy said he would name a campaign committee next week. He also confirmed an earlier published report that the committee chairwoman would be Aleesa Allison.

[8]The mayor listed three main goals if re-elected:
—A new City Hall building.
—A new comprehensive zoning plan for the 21st century.
—Pay raises for City Council members.

[9]"I am confident of victory," he concluded.

1. _____

_____

2. _____

_____

3. _____

_____

4. _____

_____

5. _____

_____

6. _____

_____

7. _____

_____

8. _____

_____

9. _____

_____

# CHAPTER SEVEN

# COVERING SPEECHES

A task certain to fall to most beginning journalists early in their news work is that of covering a speech. Many important stories are generated by speeches, and the few skills needed to cover them well are essential.

The more you know about the speaker in advance the better off you are. If you have researched the person, you will know if he or she departs from a previous position or merely repeats the old.

Find a place where you can see and hear the speaker clearly. This means sitting up front. Take more than one pen or pencil; have a backup in case one runs out of ink or if the lead breaks. Use a tape recorder if that would be appropriate to the situation. Listen carefully and take plenty of notes.

Because you probably will not be able to jot down every word the speaker says, you will have to decide which points are most important. Trust your judgment. If a certain part of the speech sounds important to you, then it probably will be important to your readers, too. In time your confidence in this area will increase. You may have to create your own quick note-taking system. In time, taking notes at speeches will become second nature to you. You will find that notes at speeches are easier to take than in interviews because the reporter doesn't have to worry about eye contact with the source.

Take notes throughout the speech. Many beginners take notes only until they have enough for a story, so they often miss important points that come near the end of the speech. Listen, also, during any question-and-answer sessions, which often are more newsworthy than the speech itself.

If you are unclear about any of the speaker's points, don't hesitate to try to find him or her after the speech to obtain clarification. If you cannot do that, leave out those parts in your news story.

In writing the story, remember this important point: Do not merely report that someone spoke. Instead, tell what the person said. Summarize his or her main points in the lead. You will never see this in a professional newspaper: President Bush today addressed Congress. The professional would, of course, recount the president's main point or points: President Bush today asked Congress to help reduce spending and to find new ways to finance the government. Tell what he said, not merely that he spoke.

Don't write: The president of the Chamber of Commerce spoke Friday, Nov. 21, to the fourth-period economics class.

Write: America's economy is growing and strong, the president of the Chamber of Commerce said Friday, Nov. 21.

After the lead, the story itself should be a mixture of direct quotes, paraphrased material and partial quotes. Don't rely too heavily on any one sort of quote. Mix them up.

Most speech stories should tell where, when and to whom the speaker spoke. Usually, however, this does not come in the lead.

Some stories require that the reporter give the size of the crowd. Don't try to estimate it yourself. Ask the police. Or the people who set up the chairs. Or someone who knows what the capacity of the auditorium or stadium is.

## Exercise 1

This is the text of a short speech delivered to the Student Council Friday, Nov. 21. The speaker is Shirley Manchester. She is editor of the Ourtown Press, a daily newspaper. The title of her speech is, ''The Role of the First Amendment in American Life.'' Write a story based on this text.

> I am very pleased to be here this afternoon, and I thank you for the invitation. I am a graduate of this school, as well as of State University, and it is always pleasant to come back.
>
> I want to talk about the First Amendment to the Constitution. That's the one that guarantees freedom of the press. It also, by the way, guarantees your freedom of religion and your right to peaceable assembly. Sometimes, I think, when people hear journalists talking about the First Amendment, they forget how much it has in it and they just think ''there go the newspaper people again, hollering about freedom of the press.'' The truth is, the First Amendment plays a key role in the quality of American life, not just in the quality of its journalism.
>
> What disturbs me, however, are the signs that the American people have stopped believing in the First Amendment. I saw a poll that says 80 percent of the American people favor a law requiring, for example, that newspapers give equal coverage to both major party candidates in a presidential race. I think we should, too, but it is our history and custom in this country for the government not to interfere in the business of the press. It is distressing to think that the people feel they need a law to make the press do what it always has done without a law.
>
> In another case, a group of college students took the First Amendment and wrote it up to make it look like a petition to the government. Then they showed it to people at a shopping mall and asked them to sign it. Most people refused, calling it ''a radical idea.'' Yes, the First Amendment is a radical idea. But it's the backbone of our way of life, and we would not survive as a nation without it.
>
> Thank you again for inviting me.

## Exercise 2

Below are the leads to five speech stories. Explain what is right or wrong about each one.

a. State University Football Coach Moon Whittaker addressed an Ourtown High School assembly on the day before Homecoming and the Dixie Conference championship game.

_____

_____

_____

_____

b. Mr. James Toland, assistant registrar at State University, told members of the Future Teachers Association Wednesday, Jan. 3, that unless the people are willing to pay more taxes, the university may have to eliminate its teacher training programs. He spoke in Room 222 at 3:30 p.m.

_____

_____

_____

_____

c. "I know I can count on all of you to help me in my campaign to eliminate littering on our campus."

_____

_____

_____

_____

d. At the assembly at the auditorium Thursday, Dec. 1, Mr. Stone, the principal, introduced the speaker, state Sen. Marcia Bucklin.

_____

_____

_____

e. Ourtown High School faces a crisis next year if students' performances on standardized test scores continue to fall, a state official warned Tuesday, Nov. 2.

_____

_____

_____

## Exercise 3

Here is the text of a speech given before a school assembly in the auditorium on Wednesday, Dec. 11. The speaker is Jules Baldwin. He is an English professor at State University. The title of his speech is "The Literacy Crisis in American High Schools." Write a story based on the previously given information and the following text of his speech.

Hi! I'm so used to sleepy college students that it's good to come before a group of wide-awake high schoolers. Thanks for inviting me. I hope to see some of you at State U. in the next few years, maybe even in my classes. I can't guarantee any of you A's but I guarantee you I'll give it my best shot.

Not all of you will make it to college, of course. Some of you will not even get out of high school. The reason is that our educational system has failed you. That and television. The truth is, and I am sad to be the one to say it, especially after that nice round of applause, the truth is that your generation has lost touch with our language and with the printed word. You don't read or write as much as you should. We, in education, have known this for a long time. But we have sat on our hands and done nothing about it. We should have been forcing you to read two books a week and to write term papers and research papers in every class. But we didn't—and now many of you are paying the price.

It isn't just here, of course. It's this way all over the country, and it's getting worse every day. Part of the problem is television. Well, not television, but the way you use television. Used properly, TV is a wonderful educational tool. But if we just sit in front of it for eight hours a day and turn our minds off, well, soon our minds turn to oatmeal. I urge you to read more and watch TV less. When I was your age I had a novel going all the time. I would carry it with me, and I even used to try to read a few lines while I was in the car waiting for the red light to change. I'm not saying read when you're driving. But find a place in your lives for the printed word.

A democracy demands well-informed citizens, citizens who know the issues and how to vote. If people don't read, especially newspapers, then they are not informed and can be easily manipulated by charismatic national leaders. Our democracy depends on you. Get yourselves ready. Read!

_____

_____

_____

_____

_____

_____

_____

_____

_____

_____

_____

_____

_____

_____

_____

_____

_____

_____

_____

_____

_____

_____

_____

_____

_____

_____

_____

## Exercise 4

A state penitentiary convict, wearing a mask so as not to be identified, speaks to an assembly Tuesday, May 2. This is the text of his talk. Write a story based on this text. The convict is identified as ''Mr. Smith,'' although that is not his real name. At the conclusion of his presentation, he is returned to prison.

There was a time when I was just like you. I went to classes and football games and dances. I got pretty good grades, too. But getting good grades is too much like hard work, so I stopped studying and started hanging around with a group of dropouts. They were having a lot of fun, so I dropped out, too.

That was the worst thing I had ever done. That was really a dumb, dumb mistake. I got a job pumping gas. Talk about hard work. That made studying seem like fun. It was too hard for me. So one night after I closed up, I just took the money from the cash register. I think it was about $67. Big deal, eh? Of course, I got caught. The next day. But they went easy on me. I got fired and put on probation. I could have, even then, gone back to school and finished my diploma. But by now I was pretty smart. I know that if I planned it right, I could steal for a living. So one night, me and another guy held up a liquor store. Then we ran in opposite directions. I thought they would only go for one of us, and naturally I thought it would be the other guy. But the cops chased both of us.

This time they didn't go easy. No breaks. I was found guilty and sentenced to three to five years in the state pen. I've been there three years now, and I hope to get a parole soon. If I do, you can bet I'm not going to mess around any more. Being in prison is no fun.

# WRITING
# FEATURE STORIES

Some young journalists feel stifled by the structure and rules that go with straight newswriting. So they prefer feature writing. Features can be—must be—more creative, more dramatic, more colorful than straight news.

But the newswriting rulebook can't be tossed out entirely just becase a story is a feature instead of straight news. The rules of attribution still apply. Opinion occasionally creeps into a feature story but that doesn't mean a feature is an editorial or a crusade.

It is true, however, that feature writing is freer of structural rules than are straight, inverted-pyramid stories. There is nothing in feature writing comparable to the inverted-pyramid sketch. Journalists can't draw a picture of a feature's structure. Features come in all sizes and shapes. They may have surprise endings or anecdotal beginnings. They may include scenes and dialogue. Many need endings. They can be two paragraphs or 200 paragraphs long. Some are written in first person. Some are treated prominently as center spreads in professional and student publications.

Features are about holidays, historical anniversaries, interesting people, unusual pets, unusual hobbies, unusual classes or class projects. They are about the teacher who is retiring or about the new teacher on the faculty. They profile the international exchange students and they tell us about the star athlete trying to decide which college scholarship to accept. They take us behind the scenes of a class play and they put us on the bus with the band and its 1,000-mile trip to a bowl game. Features show us haunted houses at Halloween and explain religious traditions during Hanukkah and Christmas.

They show the mood in the locker room at halftime and on the bench during a football game.

Features require the same kind of reporting as that involved in straight news: interviewing, reading, researching. They usually require more thought and planning before the writing begins. Straight news stories in inverted-pyramid style have a built-in structure and logic that provide the writer a place to start formulating the story. Features are harder to write because they are, indeed, less structured. They may be more fun for the writer, but that doesn't make them easier. And they have to be just as factual as the straight news story.

Most feature stories emphasize people, and it is perfectly acceptable to describe them. You wouldn't include description of City Council members in a straight story but you might want to in doing a profile of the members. Profiles are features. One tip about profiles: Remember that if you ask enough questions, every person in the world can become the subject of a feature. Everyone has interesting stories to tell if the questions bring them out.

The following exercises will help you to better understand feature writing.

## Exercise 1

Evaluate each of the following feature story leads. Which ones make you curious about the rest of the story? Which ones do not? Why?

a. It was Wednesday, Jan. 2, 1991.

_____

_____

_____

b. Dolores Thompson's mind was filled with sunny thoughts that April day. She was to be married soon, and life had taken on a rosy glow. Then her car missed a curve—and nothing has been the same since.

_____

_____

_____

c. He's a small man, about 4 feet 11 inches tall. He weighs maybe 95 pounds when he's soaking wet. And he's soaking wet most of the time.

_____

_____

_____

d. As the room filled with her classmates, Sara Jane Black could feel her confidence crumbling.

_____

_____

_____

e. Through the inky darkness, a shot rang out.

_____

_____

_____

f. If you think it's noisy in the city, try visiting a farm once.

_____

_____

_____

g. The door opened and in walked Lute, all 6 feet 8 inches of him.

_____

_____

_____

h. Have you seen the new painting in Mr. Slote's office?

_____

_____

_____

i. Lights! Camera! Action!

_____

_____

_____

j. As the immortal Bard wrote, "All the world's a stage."

_____

_____

_____

## Exercise 2

Here are five straight-news leads. Rewrite each one into a feature-type lead.

a. The City Council on Monday passed an ordinance designed to save Ourtown's elm trees from disease.

_____

_____

_____

_____

b. Ourtown High School won the Dixie Conference championship Friday night, defeating Smithville 3–0 on a 45-yard field goal with 10 seconds left in the game.

_____

_____

_____

_____

c. OHS Principal Roger Malone announced this week that he was resigning to pursue a doctoral degree at State University.

_____

_____

_____

_____

d. The OHS Student Council met Friday, Nov. 22, to elect new officers.

_____

_____

_____

_____

e. The OHS Spanish Club has decided to disband because of lack of interest.

_____

_____

_____

_____

## Exercise 3

Write a feature story using the information below.

Senior Tammy Jefferson has won the state baton twirling championship.

She won it last month in competition at State University.

She had won a regional competition earlier at OHS.

The championship carries with it a $5,000 scholarship to State U.

Tammy has been twirling the baton since she was 4 years old.

Over the years, she has won 150 trophies.

Her family long ago ran out of space to display them all, so many are stored in the basement or garage.

In an interview, Tammy had this to say: ''I was really thrilled when I heard the judge call my name as the winner. I thought I had really fouled up when I dropped the baton during one routine. But apparently that didn't hurt me a lot. I've had a lot of fun with baton twirling in my life. But I think I've had it with it now.''

''When I get to State U., I just want to study and work hard. I won't have time for this after that.''

''But I will be involved a little because I have three younger sisters who twirl the baton, and they sort of look up to me for help. So I'll continue to help them, of course.''

Tammy practiced every day for six months before winning the state championship.

''But no more for me,'' she said.

_____

_____

_____

_____

_____

_____

_____

_____

_____

_____

_____

_____

_____

_____

_____

_____

_____

_____

2. _____

_____

_____

_____

_____

_____

_____

3. _____

_____

_____

_____

_____

_____

_____

_____

_____

4. _____

_____

_____

_____

_____

_____

_____

5. _____

_____

_____

_____

_____

_____

_____

_____

## Exercise 9

Read an issue of a local commercial newspaper. List the different types of features handled in the paper. What characteristics make each story a feature? How do features differ from straight news stories?

_____

_____

_____

_____

_____

_____

_____

_____

_____

_____

_____

_____

_____

_____

_____

_____

_____

_____

_____

_____

_____

_____

_____

_____

_____

_____

_____

# WRITING SPORTS
# STORIES

It is not only athletes who know the "thrill of victory and the agony of defeat."
That describes sportswriters, too. They often are the best writers on the staff.
Once in a while they're the worst, especially when they overuse trite expressions
or cliches—bang the apple, split the uprights, sizzle the nets, and so on. Sports
stories should be written in plain English. A special language is not required.
Special terminology (note the difference) is. Legitimate sports terminology—
such as *shotgun, seam,* and *bump and run,* all football terms—must by understood
and used correctly by the writer. Figures of speech are fine, but not the old,
tired ones. Call the football the football, not the pigskin.

Good sportswriting reflects the drama, color and excitement of the event.
Sports events have these elements built in. The writer needs to capture them
and convey them to readers. A problem is that often the reader saw the event,
in person or on television. So the sportswriter has a difficult audience, one
that expects something new. So sportswriters often just skim the statistics and
play-by-play in favor of interviews with coaches and players or interpretation
of controversial calls and plays. A little of this goes a long way: Jones hits a 3-
2 curve into shallow left but Smith let it get past him. As Jones took second,
Hanson advanced from third to home. In the next inning. . . . (Yawn.) Who
scored, who was the winning pitcher, and so on, has to be in the story somewhere. But the emphasis should be on players' reactions, impact of the game
on the championship picture and the like.

Sportswriters are free to interpret the game. They are permitted more leeway
than the straight-news writer. If the game was decided on a field goal in the

second quarter, the writer is free to say so. After all, he or she was there and saw it happen. Sportswriters tend to be witnesses to what they're writing about more than straight-news writers. The City Hall reporter would have to ask someone to verify key elements in a story. Does this action mean a tax increase? Sportswriters know the facts because, often, they saw their stories happen.

Sportswriters can't be cheerleaders for the teams they follow. This is literally and figuratively true. In the press box, literally no cheering is allowed. Cover a major college football game from the press box, for instance, and you will find yourself in an eerie silence. With most of the crowd noise blocked out, the writers concentrate on the game, taking careful notes and forming and re-forming their leads as the game progresses. The only sound is that of a public address system announcer providing the writers with statistics, yard lines, etc. The sportswriter cannot be a fan. He or she has to remain objective about the team and not get caught up in its fortunes. In their hearts, most writers pull for the team they're covering. And maybe they do in their editorial columns, too. But not in sports stories. Games certainly are covered from the viewpoint of the writer's team or school. Win or lose, the emphasis is on the writer's team. But that is not the same as cheering for that team in writing.

## Exercise 1

Test your overall sports knowledge and answer the following quiz.

a. If someone scores a hat trick, what sport is he playing?

_____

_____

b. If you're a wideout, what sport and position are playing?

_____

_____

c. If you're in the squared circle, what sport are you playing?

_____

_____

d. If your perfect score is 300, what sport are you playing?

_____

_____

e. If a team is one of the Final Four, what sport is that?

_____

_____

f. If you have 92 and your opponent has 86 and you lose, what sport are you participating in?

_____

_____

g. In what sports is a three-point play possible?

_____

_____

h. If close counts, what game is being played?

_____

_____

i. If you're in the penalty box, what sport are you playing?

_____

_____

j. If you call an audible, what sport and position are you playing?

_____

_____

k. If the coach gives you the take sign, what are you doing and in what sport?

_____

_____

l. If you're playing pepper, what sport are you in?

_____

_____

m. If the score is love-15, what sport is being played?

_____

_____

n.  If your time is 15 seconds, what race did you run?

_____

_____

o.  If you won the trifecta, what did you do?

_____

_____

p.  If you're a picador, what sport are you involved in?

_____

_____

q.  If you're sacked, what sport and position are you playing?

_____

_____

r.  If you pilfer a sack, what did you do in what sport?

_____

_____

s.  If you're a coach and get a T while your team is on D, what sport is that and what happened?

_____

_____

t.  If you use a quiver, what sport are you participating in?

_____

_____

## Exercise 2

Here is another quiz to test your sports knowledge.

a.  If you need binoculars and a notebook and you're in the woods, what sport is that?

_____

_____

b.  If you have good hang time, what are you doing in what sport?

_____

_____

_____

_____

c.  If the game you play has three periods, what sport is it?

_____

_____

_____

d.  If you're a coxswain in a scull, what are you doing?

_____

_____

_____

e.  If you score a turkey, what sport are you participating in?

_____

_____

_____

f.  If you need a broom to play, what sport is that?

_____

_____

_____

g.  If it's downhill all the way, what sport is that?

_____

_____

_____

h.  If the champion goes to the Rose Bowl, what conference is it?

_____

_____

_____

i.  If you hit a shuttlecock (sometimes called a birdie), what sport are you playing?

_____

_____

_____

j.  If forwards can score but guards can't and the game is in rural Iowa, what sport is being played?

_____

_____

_____

k.  If you're in the bullpen, what position do you play in what sport?

_____

_____

_____

l.  If a handicap helps you win, what sport are you playing?

_____

_____

_____

m.  If the game is at match point, what stage of what game are you at?

_____

_____

_____

n.  If you ride a sulky, what are you doing in what sport?

_____

_____

_____


o.  If pins are involved, what sport is being played?

_____

_____

_____


p.  If goaltending is legal, what sport is that?

_____

_____

_____


q.  If goaltending is illegal, what sport is that?

_____

_____

_____


r.  If each side has 15 players, what sport is being played?

_____

_____

_____


s.  If blue chippers are involved, what sport is that?

_____

_____

_____


t.  If you're in the paint, what are you doing in what sport?

_____

_____

_____

# Exercise 3

The following list are the nicknames of university teams. Which university does each one represent?

Horned Frogs _____

Sooners _____

Red Raiders _____

Lobos _____

Cornhuskers _____

Tar Heels _____

Zips _____

Green Wave _____

Cyclones _____

Fighting Irish _____

Golden Gophers _____

Nittany Lions _____

Demon Deacons _____

Blue Devils _____

Buckeyes _____

Longhorns _____

Jayhawks _____

Hurricanes _____

Sun Devils _____

Hawkeyes _____

Razorbacks _____

Golden Bears _____

Spartans _____

Miners _____

Owls _____

Terps (Terrapins) _____

Cardinal _____

Aztecs _____

Orangemen _____

(Fightin') Hoosiers _____

# Exercise 4

Again, these nicknames represent university teams. Write the university name for each one.

Thundering Herd _____

Black Bears _____

Forty-Niners _____

Shockers _____

Golden Flashes _____

Rainbow Warriors _____

Big Green _____

Salukis _____

Crimson Tide _____

Governors _____

Chippewas _____

Fightin' Blue Hens _____

Rattlers _____

Palidans _____

Crusaders _____

Vandals _____

Minutemen _____

Blue Raiders _____

Delta Devils _____

Grizzlies _____

Racers _____

Mean Green _____

Lumberjacks _____

Ducks _____

Quakers _____

Boilermakers _____

Spiders _____

Scarlet Knights _____

Fighting Gamecocks _____

Gobblers _____

## Exercise 5

Below are some trite, overused sports words and phrases. Translate them into plain, understandable English.

bang the apple _____

split the uprights _____

toe the ball _____

hot corner _____

burn the nets _____

scoreless tie _____

gridiron _____

thinclads _____

cagers _____

grapplers _____

circuit clout _____

coveted trophies _____

pilfered sack _____

oblate spheroid _____

net tilt _____

hoop battle _____

oval _____

maples _____

paydirt _____

bingle _____

snag the aerial _____

chapter _____

canto _____

stanza _____

the D _____

charity toss _____

pigskin _____

tanksters _____

hoopsters _____

mailcarrier _____

## Exercise 6

Below is a list of words sportswriters often substitute for "defeat." Circle those that you believe are inappropriate in a sports story.

| | | | |
|---|---|---|---|
| crush | rip | kill | ruin |
| destroy | murder | gouge | slay |
| wreck | down | edge | upend |
| devastate | beat | trounce | bury |
| wallop | nail | rout | annihilate |
| clobber | bomb | upset | rock |
| beat up | punch | put away | surprise |
| pummel | poke | | |

## Exercise 7

List the names of all the teams in the National Football League. Note there are two conferences—the National and the American Conference.

_____

_____

_____

_____

_____

_____

_____

_____

_____

_____

_____

_____

_____

_____

_____

_____

_____

_____

## Exercise 8

List the names of all the Major League baseball teams. Note there are two leagues—the National and the American League.

_____

_____

_____

_____

_____

_____

_____

_____

_____

_____

_____

_____

_____

## Exercise 9

List the names of all the teams in the National Basketball Association. Note there are two conferences—the Eastern and the Western Conference.

_____

_____

_____

_____

_____

_____

_____

_____

_____

_____

_____

_____

_____

_____

_____

_____

_____

_____

_____

## Exercise 10

List the names of all the teams (universities) in the Big Eight Conference.

_____

_____

_____

_____

_____

_____

## Exercise 11

List the names of all the teams in the Pacific 10 Conference.

_____

_____

_____

_____

_____

_____

## Exercise 12

List the names of all the teams in the Southwest Conference.

_____

_____

_____

_____

_____

_____

## Exercise 13

List the names of all the teams in the Southeastern Conference.

_____

_____

_____

_____

_____

_____

## Exercise 14

List the names of all the teams in the Ivy League.

_____

_____

_____

_____

_____

_____

_____

## Exercise 15

List the names of all the teams in the Western Athletic Conference.

_____

_____

_____

_____

_____

_____

_____

## Exercise 16

List the names of all the teams in the Atlantic Coast Conference.

_____

_____

_____

_____

_____

_____

## Exercise 17

List the names of all the teams in the Big 10 Conference.

_____

_____

_____

_____

_____

_____

## Exercise 18

List the names of all the teams in the Missouri Valley Conference.

_____

_____

_____

_____

_____

_____

## Exercise 19

Make a list of all the schools that your school competes against in athletics. List each opponent's nickname/mascot and colors. List any other pertinent data, such as the name of the opponent's stadium. Determine if boys' and girls' teams use the same nickname or not (Warriors and Warriorettes, for example). Think of this list as an aid to next year's sports staff.

_____

_____

_____

_____

_____

# CHAPTER TEN

# WRITING EDITORIALS

Editorials represent the opinion functions of the media. They express the position and viewpoints of the publication or TV/radio station. Some student publications do not consider editorials to be representative of the total staff viewpoint, or a majority viewpoint. In those papers, editorials are signed. When editorials are not signed, they are considered to be the newspaper's position, not that of a single writer. Some student publications feel it essential to give both sides on all issues, and will have ''pro'' and ''con'' editorials on each topic selected.

Whatever your policy, editorial writing is not something to be taken lightly. Seldom can an editorial be written without doing a considerable amount of homework—research, interviewing, studying.

There are many types of editorials. Here are some of them. Editorials can be written to:

- explain a policy, decision or action.
- persuade students to take a course of action or respond to a situation.
- answer rumors, often-asked questions or major concerns.
- warn readers of an action that could result if certain responses or efforts are or are not made.
- criticize an action, lack of action, performance or event.
- praise those who have accomplished significant tasks or received awards.
- entertain or take a light or humorous look at an event from which your readers can learn.
- lead opinion formation around an issue.

Editorials generally consist of an *introduction* (background information to set the stage and assure the reader will understand the topic); *reaction* (the opinion of the publication or writer); *details* (to support the position); and *conclusion* (the publication's or writer's recommendations to support the reaction).

Following is a statement of editorial writing principles created by the National Conference of Editorial Writers. It contains many important thoughts that should be applied to all editorial writers.

---

### The NCEW's
### BASIC STATEMENT OF PRINCIPLES

Editorial writing is more than another way of making money. It is a profession devoted to the public welfare and to public service. The chief duty of its practitioners is to provide the information and guidance toward sound judgments that are essential to the healthy functioning of a democracy. Therefore, editorial writers owe it to their integrity and that of their profession to observe the following injunctions:

1. The editorial writer should present facts honestly and fully. It is dishonest to base an editorial on half-truth. The writer should never knowingly mislead the reader, misrepresent a situation, or place any person in a false light. No consequential errors should go uncorrected.

2. The editorial writer should draw fair conclusions from the stated facts basing them upon the weight of evidence and upon the writer's considered concept of the public good.

3. The editorial writer should never use his or her influence to seek personal favors of any kind. Gifts of value, free travel and other favors that can compromise integrity, or appear to do so, should not be accepted.

The writer should be constantly alert to conflicts of interest, real or apparent, including those that may arise from financial holdings, secondary employment, holding public office or involvement in political, civic or other organizations. Timely public disclosure can minimize suspicion.

Editors should seek to hold syndicates to these standards.

The writer, further to enhance editorial page credibility, also should encourage the institution he or she represents to avoid conflicts of interest, real or apparent.

4. The editorial writer should realize that the public will appreciate more the value of the First Amendment if others are accorded an opportunity for expression. Therefore, voice should be given to diverse opinions, edited faithfully to reflect stated views. Targets of criticism—whether in a letter, editorial, cartoon or signed column—especially deserve an opportunity to respond; editors should insist that syndicates adhere to this standard.

5. The editorial writer should regularly review his or her conclusions. The writer should not hesitate to consider new information and to revise conclusions. When changes of viewpoint are substantial, readers should be informed.

6. The editorial writer should have the courage of well-founded convictions and should never write anything that goes against his or her conscience. Many editorial pages are products of more than one mind, and sound collective judgment can be achieved only through sound individual judgments. Thoughtful individual opinions should be respected.

7. The editorial writer always should honor pledges of confidentiality. Such pledges should be made only to serve the public's need for information.

8. The editorial writer should discourage publication of editorials prepared by an outside writing service and presented as the newspaper's own. Failure to disclose the source of such editorials is unethical, and particularly reprehensible when the service is in the employ of a special interest.

9. The editorial writer should encourage thoughtful criticism of the press especially within the profession, and promote adherence to the standards set forth in this statement of principles.

## Exercise 1

You have been named editor of your school newspaper. You are writing an editorial for the first issue of the school year. This editorial will set the tone and spirit for your publication. It must assure readers that you have a clear concept of the role of the student press in your school. Write an editorial that will answer the following questions.

- What subjects will be appropriate for editorial coverage (scope)?
- Will the editorials be signed by the staff or not?
- Will the editorials be considered as the viewpoint of the newspaper as a whole, or just the writer?
- How will you treat letters to the editor?
- How will you deal with controversial issues?
- What is your paper's position on gossip?
- What are your goals for the school and how will your paper support achieving them?

_____

_____

_____

_____

_____

_____

_____

_____

_____

_____

_____

_____

_____

_____

_____

_____

_____

_____

_____

_____

_____

_____

_____

_____

_____

_____

_____

_____

_____

_____

_____

_____

_____

_____

_____

_____

_____

_____

_____

_____

_____

_____

_____

_____

_____

_____

_____

_____

_____

_____

_____

_____

_____

_____

_____

_____

_____

_____

_____

_____

## Exercise 2

Below is a feature article that appeared in *X-Ray,* the student publication of St. Charles High School in St. Charles, Illinois. After reading the feature, take any position you want on this subject and write an editorial. You may need to do research or conduct interviews to prepare for this editorial assignment.

# Teens have a 'diet of danger'

### by Fran Mauszycki

Today, teenagers eat more fast food and exercise less, which leads to high cholesterol and obesity. Teenagers today watch more television for companionship and cook the food they eat in microwaves. All of these are bad habits that are going to catch up with them when they are older in the form of heart attacks and high blood pressure.

Fast food restaurants like McDonalds, Burger King, and Wendy's are becoming teenagers' second homes. The statistics prove this, according to Paula Zahn on the ABC report "America's Kids: Diet of Danger." In the last fifteen years, pizza franchises have risen 590 percent, burger franchises have risen 100 percent, and McDonald's itself opens a franchise every 17 hours.

Because of eating this way since the 70's, teenagers are paying for all these changes in our society with high cholesterol counts, high blood pressure, and obesity. According to the report, teenagers today watch over 25 hours of television a week and are getting little exercise at school or anywhere else.

ILLINOIS IS the only state that requires daily physical exercise for school children. Very few students have physical education class everyday, and if they do, it is not the kind of exercise that builds strong bodies. Physical education and nutrition classes are at the bottom of schools' priority lists.

"Our kids have never been in worse shape, and as they grow up they will pay the price for not exercising enough and eating the wrong kinds of food," said Zahn on the report.

"School lunches are a part of the problem, providing too much fat and too much salt. Snacks add to the imbalance by providing additional fat and more sugar than young people need," said reporter Jed Duvall in the report. At lunch time, most schools sell soda pop, candy, and four or five kinds of chips that are mostly fat, salt and sugar, which are a nutritionist's nightmare.

FAST FOOD and junk foods that teenagers eat in large amounts are high in calories but usually have no nutritional value. They continue to eat these foods because they are convenient for themselves and their working parents.

Most teenagers don't eat breakfast because of lack of time, and lunch is bought at school which usually ends up as soda pop, chips, and some Hostess snack. Dinner is usually microwaved or some kind of fast food.

"We really have malnutrition among our teenagers, whether they're overweight or normal weight, they are not well nourished. They're eating, but they are not eating food. Their diet not only contains junk food, it's just about nothing else," said pediatric endocrinologist Dr. Stephanie Beling.

MOST TEENAGERS' after-school pastime is eating and watching television, which is the exact definition of a couch potato. "Lots of kids make their own dinner, find something in the refrigerator, or make dinner for whomever is around," according to school counselor Carole Siegel in the report.

This is a problem in every economic background, and it usually is the parents' fault. They either don't care or don't know what makes a good diet. In the report, too many parents are overworked, tired, or just plain bored with cooking. No one is home minding the stove.

"In the old days, there were fruits and vegetables, breads and cereals, and things like that. Now the four food groups are McDonald's, Burger King, Pizza Hut, and maybe Kentucky Fried," said Nutrition Researcher, Karen Konzelmannin in the report.

"I DON'T have time for breakfast or dinner, so lunch is my main meal. Fast food is the major staple of my diet," said junior Morna Gibbons. Junior Kris Hinz said, "I live off fast food." "I've had fast food so many times, I don't enjoy it anymore," said junior Ellen Russell. This is typical of the way teens are eating today.

Reprinted with permission. Originally published on February 3, 1989.

_____
_____
_____
_____
_____
_____
_____
_____
_____

## Exercise 3

Write an editorial based on the following information. You may take a pro or con position. You may need to do additional research at the library, or may want to interview appropriate individuals to prepare for this assignment. Keep your editorial to no more than about 200 words.

Crime, primarily in the form of vandalism, has been on an increase in your school and school neighborhood.

The parent advisory committee met last week and decided to ask local police to establish more patrols in the area.

The school board is considering closing the campus during the noon hour. It is believed that some students use this time to vandalize signs, cars and property in the area.

More than 75 incidents have been reported to police in the past five weeks. Most of these are broken windows and spray paint on fences, sidewalks and the sides of area stores and some homes.

The school property has not gone unharmed. More than 50 windows were broken last week in the rear of the school, sometime after midnight. Obscene words were spray painted on the parking lot. Restrooms have been vandalized, too.

The school board is considering placing security guards in the school to patrol throughout the day. There even has been discussion that the property should be fenced and guard dogs used after the night custodial staff leaves.

Student Council President Billi Jones has proposed a Crimestoppers program for the school. She feels that any student or area neighbor should be encouraged to call a special police number and report crime, without being required to identify him or herself.

You are aware of similar programs where callers are given code numbers, never asked for their name, and are asked to call back later to see if their call resulted in an arrest and conviction. If so, they can claim a cash reward of $100, but retain their anonymity.

Jackie Evanger, principal, has implemented a new hall pass system with faculty and student monitors placed in each stair area. Students without passes are escorted to the office.

Jay D. William, superintendent, has cautioned people not to overreact and to keep the fact in mind that vandalism is caused by a very small number of people—not all of whom are students. He strongly supports the Crimestoppers proposal.

What's your opinion?

_____

_____

_____

_____

_____

_____

_____

_____

## Exercise 4

Using the following information, write a short editorial. Take any approach or position you want. You may want to do additional research or interviews to prepare for this assignment.

The OHS school principal, Judy Gaughan, met with the Parent-Teacher-Student Advisory Committee last week for its monthly meeting, 4 p.m., in the cafeteria.

There are 18 members on the committee.

Brook Kippie, math teacher, proposed mandatory drug testing for all sports team members prior to each game.

The debate was heated. Here is part of that debate.

Kippie: ''Sports are voluntary. And conditions for playing would come as part of the dues to play. I think there is a lot of drug use here. Students often tell me of smoking and drinking at parties, and some do it just before the games.''

Gaughan: "There has only been one reported drug incident in two years—while it's probably happening, there is no hard evidence it is a problem here."

Parent Mandy Smith: "Why single out athletes? If you do it, do it for all activities—band, chess club, Student Council—all of them are voluntary participation."

Parent Ginger Katz: "I'd rather they test the teachers—they influence the students. And if they don't want to teach here because of the test, let them teach somewhere else! The logic is the same."

Foreign student Ilse Rafety: "Wait a minute. The school board has voted to require that new teachers pass a drug test before they can be hired. Why not require all teachers to take the drug test?"

Gaughan: "Please, remember that this committee is advisory. You can take your decision—if favorable—to the Board [of Education] if you want. But this policy is a prerogative."

Kippie: "What if you made it voluntary—put peer pressure on the athletes?"

Business law teacher Chuck Parker: "This whole issue is stupid—and probably will result in a few lawsuits. Shouldn't we, instead, examine our drug education programs? Beef them up! Make it a constant public relations type of campaign."

Parent Teri Shelley: "Finally, some sense. I started to think you were all bonkers!"

Kippie: "Wait a minute—we're not bonkers. We're talking lives—futures—kids are killing themselves! Athletes are role models. They are pushers' targets. How many are we going to let drift into a habit that leads to crime—or worse, death? Drugs kill and I feel that we, as leaders of the school, must take a stand. Tests are simple and easy. If someone tests positive, he or she can take a second test to confirm it. This proposal is counselling, not discrimination or punishment. Let's help these kids!"

Gaughan asked the committee to hold this issue until the next meeting which is scheduled for the first of next month. This way, students and others in the school and community can hear about the issue.

The motion was approved 9 to 7. Several of those voting stated that their votes should not be confused with their opinions. They feel the issue is important and should be discussed at the next meeting.

The committee urged interested persons to attend the meeting and express their opinions (all comments should be kept to a minimum of three minutes).

Your school newspaper is scheduled to be published two weeks before the next meeting. Your editorial will be printed in this issue. A news story will report what has been covered in this meeting and will announce the next scheduled meeting. A photo of the committee will accompany the story.

Your paper is mailed to all PTA members in addition to student distribution.

What is your opinion?

_____

_____

_____

_____

_____

_____

_____

_____

_____

_____

_____

## Exercise 5

Write a short editorial encouraging young Americans to vote in the next national election.

_____

_____

_____

_____

_____

_____

_____

_____

_____

_____

_____

_____

_____

_____

_____

_____

_____

_____

_____

_____

_____

_____

_____

_____

_____

_____

_____

_____

_____

_____

# WRITING
# HEADLINES AND
# DOING LAYOUT

Their jobs are tough, demanding and crucial. They work odd hours. And they're anonymous, rarely seeing their names in print. They are the copy editors, the professional journalists whose job is to sandpaper and polish the work of others on the newspaper staff. After a reporter turns in a story, it goes through several hands before the public sees it in print. The city editor might read and edit it, as might the managing editor. Finally, the story arrives at the copy desk. The copy editor's job is to check the story for accuracy, organization, spelling and style. Leads are often reduced, paragraphs trimmed and moved, endings added or lopped off—depending on the story. After the copy desk chief or managing editor decides where to position the story in the paper, a headline needs to be written. Of all the skills a copy editor needs, such as knowing proper grammar and being an accurate speller, none is more important than knowing how to write good headlines.

Some newspapers have very relaxed attitudes toward headlines. Copy editors at such newspapers are free to find the best five or six words to tell the story. Other papers follow strict rules about ending lines in prepositions, adjectives, etc. Each staff must decide its own policies.

Headlines should be written in a streamlined, Western Union telegram style. Their purpose is to tell and to sell the story. The headline should be bright and sassy, and it should contain the main element or elements in the story, usually those elements in the lead. Think of the headline as the super lead. All headlines need a verb. The words *a, an, and* and *the* usually are left out.

Headlines almost always are written in present tense.

It is: President Visits France

It is not: President Visited France

It is: Bears Defeat Patriots

It is not: Bears Defeated Patriots

Many newspapers prohibit lines to end in prepositions. This is wrong:

Former President of
France to Visit U.S.

Often, newspapers that prohibit headlines with lines ending in prepositions will permit such a construction in the middle line of a three-line head. Double quotes ('') never appear in headlines. Use single quotes.

Parliament
Cheers for
'Iron Lady'

Many newspapers prohibit headlines with the adjective at the end of the line and the noun that it modifies on the next line. The noun and adjective should be on the same line. This is wrong:

Arizona Faces Big
Test Against Huskies

Many publications forbid lines to end in a possessive. This is wrong:

Bush's
Tax Plan
Assailed

Punctuation is kept to a minimum. Periods are used only in abbreviations, not to end a ''sentence.'' If two complete thoughts appear in a headline, they are separated by a semicolon, not a period:

Israel Braces for Attack;
Peace Negotiation Continues

In using overlines, or kickers, remember that no one knows for sure which one readers look at first, so they have to be independent of each other. Not this:

(Overline) *Bush Says:*

(Main head) Defense Spending Needs Boost

Anyone reading the main headline and not paying attention to the overline would get the impression that the newspaper is urging an increase in defense spending. Incidentally, overlines and main heads should be set in opposite type style. That is, one should be roman and the other italic. The kicker should be half the size of the headline both vertically and horizontally.

Journalists have a "shorthand" system of referring to headlines in terms of size. An experienced journalist in a newspaper office would know, for example, that 2–36–3 means a two-column headline in 36-point type that has three lines. As a reference, note that there are 72 points in an inch. Therefore, a 36-point headline is one-half inch high and an 18-point head is one-quarter inch high. The smallest headline type in the traditional system is 12-point, going up in size in the following gradations: 14, 18, 24, 30, 36, 42, 48, 54 (rarely used), 60, 72, 84, and 96. Obviously, the bigger the story is in news value, the bigger the headline should be.

Headlines have to fit. If an article is 2 columns wide, two columns is the limit for the headline width. The headline can't pop out of the right-hand side into the next column. Many newspapers have computers that "tell" the copy editor if the headline is running too long. When writing headlines, journalists cherish short words and use abbreviations, as long as they're widely understood. For example, headline writers know the word "prejudice" in a news story can become "bias" in the headline. If a headlines writer does not have a computerized system to rely on as far as headlines and page layout are concerned, that person must rely on a headline chart or a unit count system like the one that appears in the first exercise in this chapter.

Planning on how the newspaper page elements—headlines, stories, photos—will appear on a page is known as doing layout or dummying. With the advances in computer technology and desktop publishing, "laying out" the elements of a newspaper or newsmagazine page has become easier. The basic guidelines for the editor remain the same, however, and are as follows:

- The biggest headline should be put on the most important story, and that story should be placed on the most important part of the page.
- Headlines of equal or near-equal size should not be placed beside each other.
- "Heavy" elements, such as pictures and stories with large headlines, should be arranged around the page to create a visually pleasing effect.

The following exercises will help you develop your headline-writing skills and give you hands-on practice in news judgment and page layout.

## Unit Count System

| Letter | Count | Letter | Count |
|---|---|---|---|
| Capital I | 1 | Spaces | ½ |
| Capital M,W,O | 2 | Numerals | 1 |
| All other capitals | 1½ | The numeral 1 | ½ |
| Lowercase j, l, f, t, and i | ½ | Question mark, dash | 1 |
| Lowercase w and m | 1½ | All other punctuation | ½ |
| All other lowercase letters | 1 | | |

## Exercise 1

The unit count system above is the traditional system for determining how long a headline will be once it is set in type. For instance, note how many units a capital ''M'' equals compared to a lower case ''f.'' Count each of the headlines below using this system and write the total number of units in the space provided.

Example: S c h o o l Wins High State Rating          total units    26½

Cow jumps over the moon

'Sky falling,' chicken claims

Tax measure sent to House, Senate

Bears win Super Bowl!

Baseball season

opens tomorrow

Parade, Game Highlight Homecoming

President visits Europe, Asia; next trip pondered

The Hostages: Where Are They Now?

Sooners, Longhorns clash in Cotton Bowl

## Exercise 2

Each of the headlines below has a flaw. Find the flaw and briefly explain why it is wrong.

a. New limits on
   spending asked

   _____

   _____

b. Lady Wildcats'
   streak broken

   _____

   _____

c. 35-degree drop
   in 90 minutes

   _____

   _____

d. Texas redistricting
   plan loses battle

   _____

   _____

e. Crash course may
   help in prevention
   of food poisoning

   _____

   _____

f. Lack of loyalty a factor
   that turns Americans
   into spies, experts say

   _____

   _____

g. Would-be victim holds suspect for police

   _____

   _____

h. Sally McBride, James
   Pulsome win crowns

   _____

   _____

i. Slay suspect in shootout

   _____

   _____

j. State braces for big
   blizzard as temps dip

   _____

   _____

## Exercise 3

The words below are too long for a headline. Find a shorter word for each one.

| Confederacy _____ | lackadaisical _____ |
|---|---|
| sightseer _____ | distant _____ |
| sedate (adj.) _____ | bridge (n.) _____ |
| professor _____ | helicopter _____ |
| receive _____ | prejudice _____ |
| recommend _____ | redistrict _____ |
| country _____ | emphasize _____ |
| Philadelphia _____ | charged _____ |
| eyewitness _____ | unemployment _____ |
| resign _____ | municipal _____ |

## Exercise 4

Again, the following words are too long for a headline. Find a shorter word for each one.

suggest _____     assistant _____

consider _____     automobile _____

narcotics _____     attempt _____

perspiration _____     relocate _____

committee _____     locate _____

television _____     discharge (v.) _____

airplane _____     display (v.) _____

Defense Department _____     neighborhood _____

assist _____     endorse _____

island _____     ensnare _____

## Exercise 5

To be used in a headline, each of the words below needs a shorter version. Replace each one with a better word.

conspiracy _____     ambassador _____

collusion _____     dirigible _____

commence _____     determine _____

prison _____     investigate _____

clergyman _____     appoint _____

hamburger _____     destroy _____

cavern _____     destiny _____

Caucasian _____     homosexual _____

bacteria _____     movie _____

dispute (n.) _____     revenue _____

## Exercise 6

Here, again, are words that are too long for a headline. Find a shorter word for each one.

| | | | |
|---|---|---|---|
| champions | _____ | exchange (v.) | _____ |
| cheer | _____ | release (v.) | _____ |
| former | _____ | promise | _____ |
| criticize | _____ | promote | _____ |
| schedule | _____ | occupation | _____ |
| consumer | _____ | obituary | _____ |
| purchase | _____ | ill-mannered | _____ |
| saxophone | _____ | eradicate | _____ |
| earthquake | _____ | nuclear weapons | _____ |
| explosion | _____ | capture | _____ |

## Exercise 7

To further sharpen your headline writing skills, find a shorter word for each of the following.

| | | | |
|---|---|---|---|
| introduce | _____ | accident | _____ |
| basement | _____ | construct | _____ |
| ceiling | _____ | manufacture | _____ |
| mountain | _____ | legislation | _____ |
| contract | _____ | select | _____ |
| relative | _____ | announce | _____ |
| veterans | _____ | triumph | _____ |
| Southeast Asia | _____ | rebellion | _____ |
| prisoner | _____ | tornado | _____ |
| consider | _____ | headquarters | _____ |

## Exercise 8

Write a 3–36–1 headline for each of the stories below. The maximum count is 28. The minimum is 26.

a. _____

How would you like to win full tuition for eight semesters to the University of Northern Iowa? Would you be excited?

Ruth Choate was when she found out that she was the winner of a chemistry scholarship.

Mr. Moberly took 10 students to Cedar Rapids on Nov. 15 and 16 where each student tried for one of the scholarships. There were five different areas and two scholarships were awarded in each area, plus two others were up for grabs.

(From the North High *Oracle,* Des Moines, Iowa)

b. _____

Student Council, now finished with Homecoming, its major fall project, is putting new ideas into action.

The council is currently working to assist the Christian Anonymous Program. President Missy Merideth explains, ''This program works with needy families in the community, securing food, clothing and other gifts.''

The Student Council will also get involved with Channel One, a program through which food donations are collected for the needy in the Rochester area.

Special committees have been set up and meet weekly before school to organize individual activities.

(From the Mayo High School *Advocate,* Rochester, Minn.)

c. _____

Seniors had the highest percentage of 90 and above grades and the lowest percentage of failures of all four classes at the end of the first six weeks grading period.

Thirty-seven percent of the senior classes' grades were 90 and above while only 6 percent were failures.

The junior class was next with 33 percent in the 90 and above range and 8 percent failures. The freshman class had 32 percent of its grades above 90 and 8 percent failures.

The sophomore class had the highest percent of failing grades at 11 percent and the smallest percent of 90 and above grades with only 29 percent.

(From the *Hoof Print,* Alamo Heights High School, San Antonio, Texas)

# Exercise 9

Write a 2–30–2 headline for each of the stories below. Your maximum count is 22, and the minimum is 20.

a. _____

_____

After a layoff lasting over a decade, National Honor Society is currently being pushed for reinstatement as a program of recognizing outstanding students at Sunset.

The organization, under the sponsorship and supervision of the National Association of Secondary School Principals (NASSP), as mentioned in its constitution, is formed ''to create enthusiasm for scholarship, to stimulate a desire to render service, to promote leadership, and to develop character in the students of the secondary school.''

The efforts began this summer through students, phone calls from parents, and the new administration. In particular, Sunset senior Bridgette Whisnant wrote a letter to National Honor Society (NHS) regarding its return to Sunset.

''If there is a student who is pushing the most, Bridgette has been the spark plug,'' said Tom Marsh, activities director.

(From the *Scroll,* Sunset High School, Beaverton, Ore.)

b. _____

_____

Sixty-six students donated blood to the American Red Cross Oct. 18. Each donor gave one pint, which will save about four to five lives.

Shelly Arndt, Sr., said, ''It makes me feel good to give my blood to help others.''

The entire process takes about 45 minutes, where the donation itself takes only 10 to 45 minutes. Each donor has to go to the five stations before giving blood. At the first station, registered nurses checked temperature and blood pressure. At the second station, a health history was completed. This made sure the blood was safe for a patient to receive.

Next, at the third station, a blood sample was taken from the ear to see if there was a problem with iron-poor blood. Before the donor could give blood, he had to drink a cup of orange juice to help prevent passing out. Finally, the donation of blood took place.

(From the *Torch,* Wichita High School South, Wichita, Kan.)

c. _____

_____

---

Applications are now being accepted from girls 13 through 19 for the Miss Texas U.S. Teen Pageant.

The Texas winner will receive $250 in cash, one-year college scholarship, and all-expense trip to the national pageant including airfare, watch, diamond pendant, color portrait, crown, banner, trophy and a host of gifts and products.

In addition to the state title, awards will be given in leadership, friendship and photogenic categories.

The Texas pageant will be held at the Amfac Hotel in Dallas. Judging is based on poise, personality, school and community involvement.

(From the *Statesman,* John Jay High School, San Antonio, Texas.)

---

## Exercise 10

Write a 2–36–2 headline for each of the stories below. The maximum count is 18, the minimum 16.

a. _____

_____

---

They're here! The latest in achievement recognition. A craze that won't stop until the last final exam. Don't delay. Start working for your academic letter today.

For the first time, East High School will honor academic achievers with a letter designed especially for this purpose. To achieve an academic letter, a student must maintain a 3.6 grade-point average for two semesters in the same year.

East and Roosevelt High became the first two schools in Des Moines to award academic letters. Roosevelt's requirements are basically the same, except that Roosevelt requires a 3.25 GPA.

(From the East High *Scroll,* Des Moines, Iowa)

b. _____

_____

---

Countywide Scholastic Aptitude Test (SAT) scores for this year's graduating class proved the highest in over 10 years despite a 14-point decrease at RHS.

English Resource Teacher Wayne Fleeger feels the decrease in scores is insignificant.

A two-section test of verbal and mathematical skills, the SAT rates each section on a point basis, considering 800 a perfect score and 200 the lowest score.

With approximately 74 percent of the class taking the test, RHS seniors scored six points below the county verbal mean, averaging 463 points. However, this year's graduating class surpassed the math section county mean by an equal amount, with an average of 529. The verbal and math averages placed Rockville seniors eighth and seventh, respectively, among all Montgomery County schools.

These standings are down from last year, when RHS placed seventh in verbal and fourth in math.

(From the *Rampage,* Rockville High School, Rockville, Md.)

---

c. _____

_____

---

Class of '99 elections were held Nov. 21.

Kip Andersen and Joann Santa-Ana ended dead even and are now co-presidents of the class of 610 students. This is the first time this has happened in the seventh grade classes.

Charles Eklund captured the vice presidency over Gretchen Smith. Mili Pena was victorious against Angela Funes for secretary; Mark Bolt beat Tony Perry for treasurer. . . .

There were a large number of students who ran for office. Because of this, preliminary elections were held to narrow the number of candidates for the Nov. 21 elections.

(From the *Bear Facts,* Lake Braddock Secondary School, Burke, Va.)

# Exercise 11

Considering what you have learned about news judgment, headlines and layout, design the front page of a school newspaper using the stories and the dummy/layout grid below. Before you begin, refer to the example of an actual newspaper dummy and the resulting front page provided on page 124.

a. A six-inch story and photo of a successful performance by the drama department of "You're a Good Man, Charlie Brown."

b. A seven-inch story and photo about five students attending a special program in Washington, D.C.

c. A six-inch story about the Jazz Band winning a top rating at a festival at a nearby college.

d. A five-inch story about students attending a medical conference at a nearby hospital.

e. A six-inch story about the DECA (Distributive Education Clubs of America) group competing successfully in a region competition.

f. A seven-inch story about tryouts for the flag team, drill team and cheerleading squad.

PAGE _____  SECTION _____

| ½ | | | | | 21 |
| 1 | | | | | 20 |
| 2 | | | | | 19 |
| 3 | | | | | 18 |
| 4 | | | | | 17 |
| 5 | | | | | 16 |
| 6 | | | | | 15 |
| 7 | | | | | 14 |
| 8 | | | | | 13 |
| 9 | | | | | 12 |
| 10 | | | | | 11 |
| 11 | | | | | 10 |
| 12 | | | | | 9 |
| 13 | | | | | 8 |
| 14 | | | | | 7 |
| 15 | | | | | 6 |
| 16 | | | | | 5 |
| 17 | | | | | 4 |
| 18 | | | | | 3 |
| 19 | | | | | 2 |
| 20 | | | | | 1 |
| 21 | | | | | |

**The numbers along the sides represent inches.**

## Exercise 12

Practice your layout and news-judgment skills again. Draw a front-page layout for the elements below. Use the dummy provided below. Your newspaper flag (name) is three columns wide and you have one photograph to use.

a. A nine-inch story with a photo of the death of a sophomore student in an automobile accident.

b. A five-inch story about the death, from cancer, of a substitute teacher.

c. An eight-inch story announcing tighter requirements for graduation.

d. A nine-inch story previewing a performance of "The Tempest" by the drama department.

e. A nine-inch story announcing that members of the Chinese Embassy are going to visit your school to learn how it runs.

PAGE _____    SECTION _____

| ½ | | | | | 21 |
| 1 | | | | | 20 |
| 2 | | | | | 19 |
| 3 | | | | | 18 |
| 4 | | | | | 17 |
| 5 | | | | | 16 |
| 6 | | | | | 15 |
| 7 | | | | | 14 |
| 8 | | | | | 13 |
| 9 | | | | | 12 |
| 10 | | | | | 11 |
| 11 | | | | | 10 |
| 12 | | | | | 9 |
| 13 | | | | | 8 |
| 14 | | | | | 7 |
| 15 | | | | | 6 |
| 16 | | | | | 5 |
| 17 | | | | | 4 |
| 18 | | | | | 3 |
| 19 | | | | | 2 |
| 20 | | | | | 1 |
| 21 | | | | | |

**The numbers along the sides represent inches.**

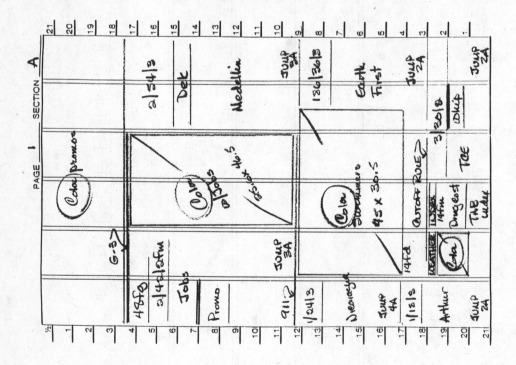

## Exercise 13

Although many commercial newspapers still use the traditional dummy to lay out the newspaper page, many publications—including student newspapers—are now using computer technology, namely desktop publishing, to produce newspapers, news magazines, and yearbooks. Below is a template, a grid with page and style elements, representative of those found with desktop publishing software programs, such as PageMaker (Aldus Corporation). Using desktop publishing saves hours of time normally spent on layout.

# Masthead

## 36pt. headline placeholder

*18pt. subhead placeholder*

### 24pt. column headline placeholder

**This is a 12pt. bold byline placeholder**

This is a 12pt. body text placeholder composed of Times Roman set flush left

*This is a 12pt. caption placeholder of Times Roman italic*

Illustration courtesy of Thomas Bivins, University of Oregon

Note: On this template, ''masthead'' refers to the flag of the publication.

If your paper is produced using desktop publishing, determine the elements and placement of those elements in terms of the ''master page'' or template available on the program you use.

# USING PHOTOS EFFECTIVELY

Effective use of photographs in publications allows readers to see the event about which you are writing. They complement and supplement your story.

Photos in a publication are used to:

- capture a reader's attention.
- inform—to show what is happening.
- entertain.
- link the reader with the feeling and emotion of a story, such as happiness, fear and sorrow.
- break up the page—as a layout device.

Photographers, while always on the alert for exciting, creative photos, work closely with reporters to cover a particular story. The assignment editor may determine that a particular event warrants sending a photographer along with the reporter. All three should discuss, ahead of time, how the story might be illustrated. To capture the right photograph, the photographer should research what has been used before (if anything) on the same or similar topic. This way, the photographer can avoid taking the same old picture again.

Photos should be selected because of their relevance to a story, their content and the composition of the picture (close-up, good action, shape, lighting). Photos have to fit the space available—columns or inches wide by inches deep, horizontal or vertical format, action facing right or left.

After a picture has been selected and the page layout determined, a cutline is written. A cutline identifies who or what is in the picture and where it was taken. Good cutlines must be able to stand alone. A reader should not have to read the story in order to understand what is in the picture. Good cutlines can include details not mentioned in the story, or just can be humorous. All cutlines should be written in the present tense. This lends a feeling of immediacy.

Cropping the photos is the next step. ''Cropping'' means getting rid of any visual clutter at the top, bottom or sides, bearing in mind what is important in the picture in relation to the news story, the cutline and the layout. To crop a picture, mark lines in the white margins of the photo (or close to the edges) using a grease pencil—sometimes called a china marker. Why use a grease pencil? Obviously, you can change your mind on crop marks easily; just wipe off the grease marks and start over. If you use a regular pencil or ballpoint pen, not only is it hard to change the crop marks, but you can permanently damage the photo. Even if you write on the back of a photo with a regular pen or pencil, you can crack the front finish of the photo. Marks may show up on the final print. Fountain pens and markers should also be avoided; ink can be absorbed into the photographic paper and ruin the original. Depending on the procedure used in your class or newspaper office, you may use a cropping/scaling device to determine the crop marks and rely on the printer to ''size'' the photo—that is, determine the percentage of enlargement or reduction necessary per the layout. The traditional method, however, is to measure and note the cropped image of the photo yourself—width by depth—and then measure the ''hole'' for the picture on the page layout. The next step involves ''sizing'' the photo using a proportion wheel, a tool commonly used in graphic arts and publishing. (See the illustration on the next page.)

## How to Use a Proportion Wheel

Take your proportion wheel and find the original width on the inside wheel—four inches, as illustrated. Now, holding the wheel firmly, locate the final width desired—in this case, two inches. Note the percentage needed for reduction is indicated as 50%. Now, holding the wheel firmly, find the original depth (7 inches, in this case) on the inside wheel. Note the finished depth is indicated as 3½ inches. If the layout calls for a different depth, you may have to adjust your crop marks accordingly and resize the photo. Changing the layout is an option if you have the flexibility and time to do so. This is more often the case with yearbook and magazine production.

After you have sized the photo, you may be instructed to write the finished size of the picture on the layout or dummy, along with carefully noting the original and final size on the back of the photo or on a tag attached to the photo. By doing this, you may reduce chances for error at the printer, assuming you have double-checked your sizing. Whether you use this procedure depends on the routine used for your newspaper and if your printer prepares the photos for reproduction. If you use desktop publishing, including a scanner, to prepare your school newspaper, you may well scan the photo in yourself. The picture is then in position when the newspaper page master (often called camera-ready copy) is printed out at the laser printer.

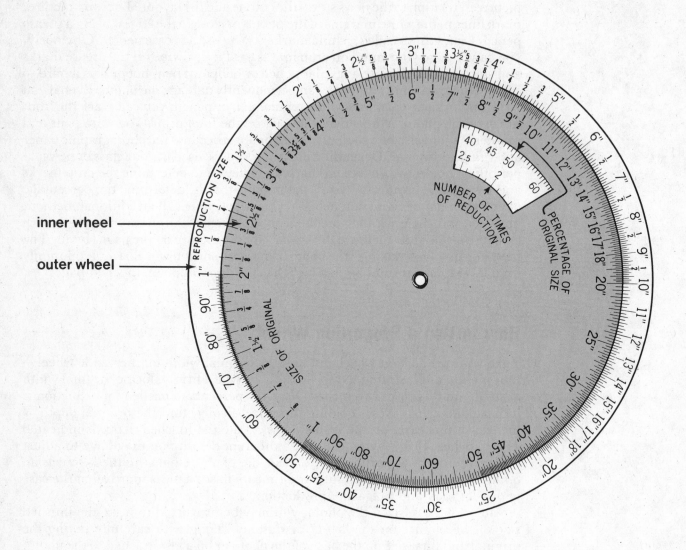

**inner wheel**

**outer wheel**

**Example**:  4 × 7 reduced to 2 × 3½ (50% reduction)

## Exercise 1

The photograph below has been cropped. Using what you have learned about the proportion wheel, find the missing dimensions for each of the following. A column width is 2″ wide with a ⅛″ gutter (space between columns).

a.  Enlarge from _____″ × _____″ to (3 columns) _____″ × _____″

b.  Reduce from _____″ × _____″ to 2″ × _____″

c.  Enlarge from _____″ × _____″ to _____″ × 12½″

## Exercise 2

Here is a photograph taken at a special event. To use the picture in your school paper, you will need to do the following.

a. Crop the picture to fit a three-column wide format. A column is 2″ wide and a gutter between columns is ⅛″.

b. Using the same picture, write a cutline based on the following information.

The Great Bicycle Race

An annual school event that is in its 10th year.

There were 40 teams this year. Student organizations and a teachers' group made up the teams.

The race weaved its way through the community and around the school property.

The race stretched 25 miles.

There were five riders for each team and each rider biked five miles.

The Key Club completed the course first. The Girls Swim Team placed second and the Chess Club came third. The teachers' team finished in 25th place.

_____

_____

## Exercise 3

This picture was taken at last night's basketball game. To use the picture in your school paper, you need to do the following.

a. Crop the picture to fit a two-column wide format. A column is 2″ wide and a gutter between columns is ⅛″.

b. Using the same picture, write a cutline based on the following information.

Debra Fox just shot a scoring basket for Ourtown High School Girls Basketball Team. They played Lincoln High School.

Game was last night, Wednesday, at 8 p.m. The game was held at Prasch gym in Lincoln.

Approximately 850 people attended.

OHS team won, 89 to 84.

Susan Birch had the highest score with 22 points.

The next game is at home. It will be held on Saturday, 2 p.m. two weeks from tomorrow. (This photo goes in Friday's paper.)

## Exercise 4

Practice your cropping and cutline skills again. To use the picture in your school paper, you need to do the following.

a. Crop the picture to eliminate the dark areas. It should be 8″ deep on your layout page. A column is 2″ wide.

b. Write a cutline for the picture using the information below.

Ourtown High School Rooster

The new mascot, Rooster II, is the successor for Rooster I. Rooster I's costume fell apart.

Rooster II was the project of the Spirit Club.

He made his first appearance at a pep rally on Friday, 3 p.m.

Rooster II will be at the OHS basketball game on Saturday.

The game begins at 8 p.m.

OHS team will play Yourtown High School Badgers at the Jones Arena.

# CREATING ADS

Advertising helps pay the cost of producing any publication. This reality is one aspect of the economic function of media. However, the other economic function of the media—and more important—is how the public learns about products, goods and services. Advertising helps stimulate the economy and publications.

School publications should never consider advertising as a contribution. Students have money to spend. In addition, they influence the decisions made at home, such as the purchase of entertainment equipment or where to dine out. Student publications are a logical place for a business or organization to advertise in order to reach a large target market.

However, local businesses don't necessarily contact publications to advertise in the paper. Few ads "walk in the door." It is the publication's responsibility to get businesses or organizations to advertise. At the scholastic level, students write the sales letters, make the cold calls (calling on businesses without prior introduction), and even develop advertising copy and layout in the cases when camera ready copy for ads is not provided by the advertiser.

One way you can persuade a business or an organization to advertise is to show a student marketing study that demonstrates the dollar impact students have on a particular business. Effective use of student marketing studies can raise significant income to produce the student publication, buy desktop publishing or darkroom equipment, take field trips, or make other improvements in the journalism program.

When it's time to prepare an ad yourself for a particular advertiser, note the following steps that should be taken:

- Do your homework. Know what products the advertiser sells that students buy and why they buy them.
- See what your advertiser's competitors are selling, and how they are selling it (the appeals used, messages, price information).
- Remember the five W's and H—who will buy the product or use the service? What is it? What will make consumers buy it and why? When, where and how can it be purchased?
- Develop your headline (the grabber) and write the copy with the customer's needs in mind ("What's in it for me?").
- Don't forget the call to action—where to get it, when and at what price.
- Be brief, clear, honest and accurate.
- Select meaningful, strong illustration (photos or art).
- Be creative.

Most ads will include these elements:

1. store name and logo
2. headline
3. strong lead-in
4. copy blocks
5. store hours, address and phone number
6. prices (sizes if important), discounts
7. dates of sale (if any)
8. illustration
9. call to action.

## Exercise 1

Bill and Sue's Entertainment Center wants to sell its product. Read the following information and create an ad for Bill and Sue's that targets students at your school. Draw a rough sketch of the ad on the dummy on page 135. The ad should be four columns wide by 12″ deep. One column is 2″ and a gutter is ⅛″. Ad copy can be written on page 136.

The product is available from Bill and Sue's Entertainment Center, 4456 South 23rd (three blocks from campus), phone 555-6868. The product is a portable CD player with high quality headset.

Your marketing research indicates that about 40 percent of the students have a similar piece of entertainment equipment. It also shows that about 28 percent plan to buy one in the current school year.

This piece of equipment is available at 30 percent off. Regular price was $179—a savings of $53.70. In addition, the customer can select a free CD album of his or her choice from the top ten albums as a bonus. They must bring the ad to the store within two weeks. The sale ends at this time.

School policy allows use of the players in the library, study halls, and, at teacher's discretion, during study periods in class.

The equipment has a belt hook so it can be strapped on when walking.

It comes with rechargeable batteries. A charger can be purchased for $8 as an option.

You have a photo of two students using the equipment in the library and a photo of a student jogging while wearing the player.

Due to the special price, the brand name of the CD player cannot be placed in the ad, but you know it is a top brand. The name does not show in the two photos.

You own a personal CD player already.

Use this logo somewhere in the ad. Make it any size you choose.

PAGE _____ SECTION _____

The numbers along the sides represent inches.

_____

_____

_____

_____

## Exercise 2

Using the information from the previous exercise, write a sales letter to Bill and Sue's Entertainment Center. Stress the value of advertising in your paper. For this exercise, you may invent survey results. The advertisement you created for Bill and Sue's will be sent along with the letter.

_____

_____

_____

_____

_____

_____

_____

_____

_____

## Exercise 3

You want Varsity Tuxedo Rentals to advertise in your school paper. Read the information below and create an advertisement for Varsity. Draw a rough sketch on the dummy provided. The ad should be three columns wide by 5″ deep. One column is 2″ and a gutter is ⅛″. Ad copy can be written on page 138 after the rough sketch.

Approximately 60 percent of the students attend the prom. Your marketing study noted that all but 10 percent of the men will rent their formal wear.

Varsity, located at 555 South Adams, phone 555-8960, has a wide selection of tuxedos, with shirts and shoes to match.

Complete package deals are available from $55 to 80. Shoe rental is $12 per pair.

Students receive a 5-percent discount for each week that they reserve ahead, up to 20 percent off rental costs.

Each student who comes to Varsity can register to win free limousine service for prom night. Two students' names will be drawn.

Visit Varsity's showroom, open 9–5 weekdays, 9–noon on Saturdays.

You have a photo of two seniors in tuxedos that can be used. You also have a quality sketch of line art showing a couple in formal wear.

Use this logo somewhere in the ad. Make it any size you choose.

# Varsity Tuxedo Rentals

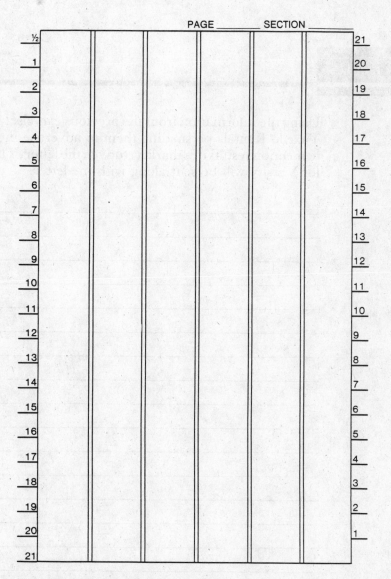

The numbers along the sides represent inches.

_____

_____

_____

_____

_____

_____

_____

_____

_____

_____

## Exercise 4

Using the information from the previous exercise, write a sales letter to Varsity Tuxedo Rentals persuading them to advertise in your paper. You may want to mention results of a market study in the letter. The advertisement you created for Varsity will be sent along with the letter.

_____

_____

_____

_____

_____

_____

_____

_____

_____

_____

_____

_____

_____

_____

# PLANNING THE YEARBOOK

Like any publication that is done well, yearbooks take considerable planning. You need to determine the size of the book, how many pages it will contain, and how the pages will look.

Yearbook layout is often classified as liberal or conservative, horizontal or vertical. Authors of various texts and each yearbook company have a variety of terms for different layout styles.

A liberal layout will have more white space on the pair of facing pages (the two pages that face the reader). A conservative layout will use most of the page, filling it with copy, headlines, photos and cutlines.

In a horizontal layout, the pages appear to flow horizontally on the pair of pages. Usually, there will be at least one dominant element that is horizontal— possibly a large photo that bleeds into the gutter or to the edges. Other elements cluster around it. The opposite is true for a vertical page. White space is kept to the outside of the pages and never trapped between elements.

There are no hard-and-fast rules to follow for yearbook layouts. To understand the many different ideas and trends in layouts, you need to become a "student" of magazines. Look at as many magazine layouts as you can. Magazines, like yearbooks, are constantly changing. The following are examples of different types of layouts.

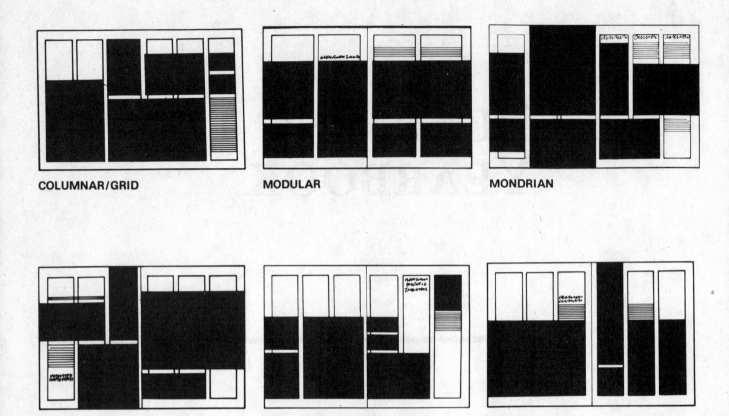

COLUMNAR/GRID          MODULAR          MONDRIAN

MOSAIC          FLOATER/ISOLATED ELEMENT          SMOKESTACK

Layouts courtesy of National Scholastic Press Association, Minneapolis, Minn. (Black areas indicate photos; lined areas, copy; blank areas, white space.)

## Exercise 1

As a member of the yearbook staff, you have the opportunity to design parts of the yearbook. On the following pages are several photographs. Select any photos you wish and design two yearbook layouts. You may use the following miniature layout sheets. Refer to photos as *a*, *b*, and so on.

You can refer to the layout samples above as your guide. But try not to design identical layouts. Remember, the samples are only that—samples. Be creative. Try to design layouts that are unique, such as a centerspread with a photo "bleeding in the gutter." You may use all the photos or just a few. You can enlarge a picture or reduce it. If you use a picture more than once, your crop marks may change. If they do, label each set of marks to coordinate with the layout number.

Be sure you crop the photos for maximum impact. Once you've determined the size you want, mark the reduction or enlargement figures on the space provided beside each picture.

Carefully indicate which areas on a layout page are pictures, headlines, copy blocks or cutlines. Number your layouts *1* and *2*.

a.  reduce/enlarge

from _____ × _____

to _____ × _____

b.  reduce/enlarge

from _____ × _____

to _____ × _____

c. reduce/enlarge

from _____ × _____

to _____ × _____

d. reduce/enlarge

from _____ × _____

to _____ × _____

e. reduce/enlarge

from _____ × _____

to _____ × _____

f. reduce/enlarge

from _____ × _____

to _____ × _____

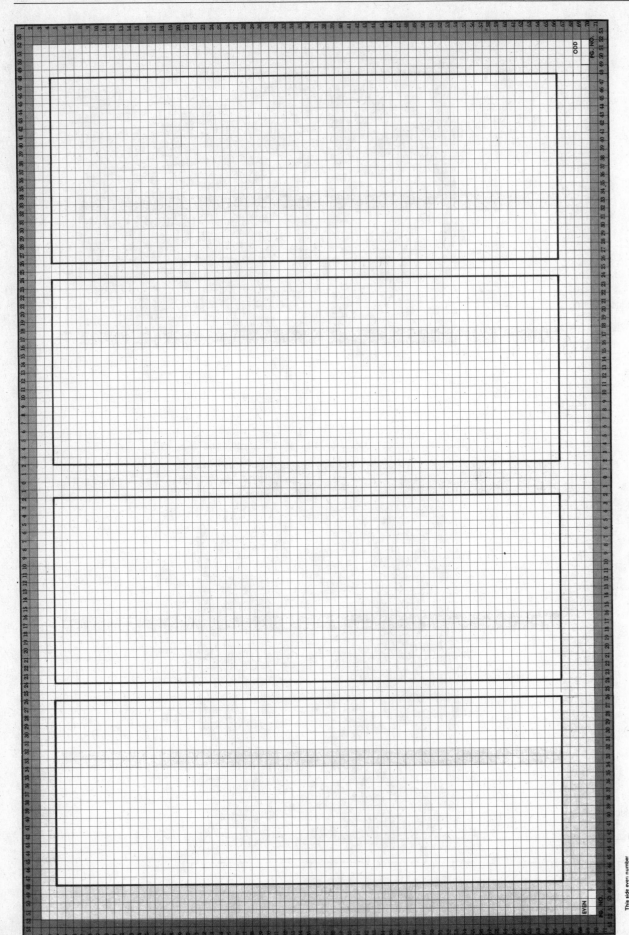

**layout sheet**

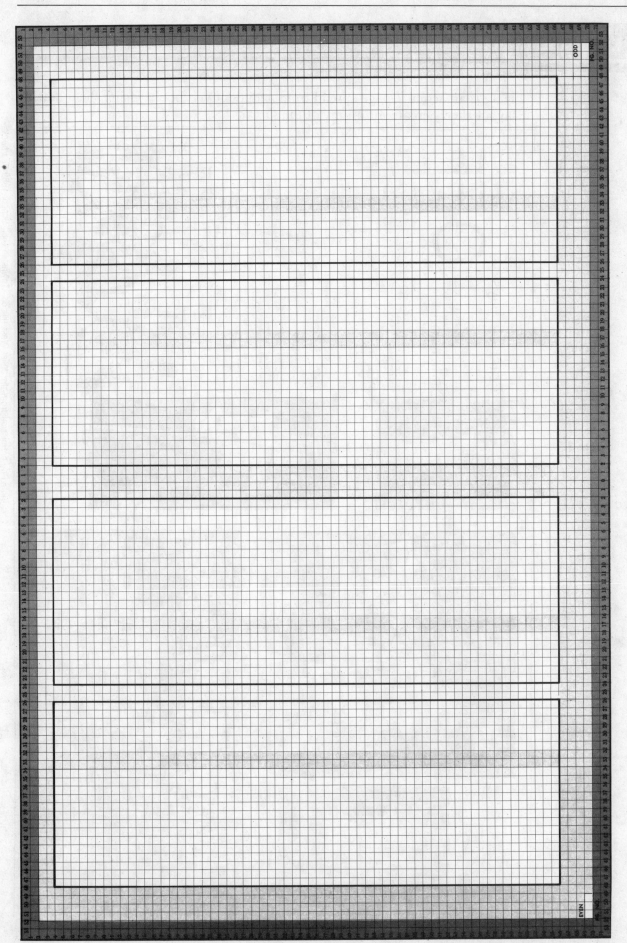

layout sheet

## Exercise 2

Here is an actual 2-page spread from a student yearbook. Using the following layout sheet, create a dummy of the spread.

# OFF

## Practice pays

### West bands and flags reap the rewards of strong commitment and dedication

Do the words dedication, practice and patience ring a bell? To approximately 100 band members, these words were repeated every day.

Besides school day practices, the band also practiced during the summer and in the evenings before competitions and home games, said director Dean Sayles.

Throughout the marching season, the band participated in five parades—of which they won first place at three—and the 20th Annual Marching Band Festival at Wheeling High School where they took first in the AA Division.

"Wheeling was the highlight of our season," said Sayles. "It surprised us that we did so well."

The group also competed at Illinois State University and University of Illinois marching competitions where they received honorable mentions.

"We were the only band to get rained on at U of I competition," said Sayles. "It had some effect on our performance."

Jazz band, a group of 16 members who played upbeat jazz, rock ballads and jazz from the '20s, '40s and '50s, performed at concerts and several basketball games.

Another early morning practicing group was orchestra.

The West and Central combined orchestra performed at two concerts of their own and participated in a string clinic hosted by West, attended by four area high schools and conducted by musicians from Northern Illinois University.

The Tiger Guard started its season by attending a summer camp then choreographing routines with the band. They performed at all home football games, parades and band competitions.

A new flag group called Winter Guard had its first successful season.

This group of 12 girls competed at Sycamore competition where they placed second and at Downers Grove North competition where they won first place and qualified for state.

"At the beginning of the season no one knew anything; they learned quickly and created a success of themselves," said senior co-captain Heidi Lesnely.

The band student teacher for the year was Kelly Markwell. Band officers included President Kevin Robertson, Vice President Eli Limacher, Secretary Verna Toma, Treasurer Jeff Dahlen and Quarter Master Rachel Gray. The black band sponsor was Stephanie Brumund and the gold band sponsor was Nikki Page.

*Tiger Guard members* are front, Heather Linn, Tata Mam; middle, Alicia Lucas, Heidi Lesnely, Chrisi Zaletel, Terri Troutman; back Michelle Alling, Kris Boese, Betsy Palmer, Kim Clay, Leigh Ann Swolley.

*Senior Betsy Palmer* leads the Tiger Guard in the Homecoming parade.

*Drum major Kevin Robertson*, a senior, conducts the band during a halftime performance.

*Sophomores Timm Chaney* and Dale Lasser pep up the crowd with their trumpet playing at a basketball game.

*Sophomore Mike Magosky* notices a mis-marked note as he practices for the winter band concert.

*Marching band members* are front, Heather Linn, Rodney Pierce, Brad Magosky, Julie Brown, Bryan Laibley, Tony Immekus, Mike Fisher, Amy Varvel, Kevin Robertson, Craig Sayles, Mike Duff, Fred King, Bill Green, Morgan Henning, Ed Hill, Jason Hergesilke, Sam Wilson, Julie Smith; second, Brian Leslie, Isaac Brooks, Alicia Lucas, Chris Zaletel, Terri Troutman, Paola Marucco, Leigh Ann Swolley, Betsy Palmer, Michelle Alling, Kris Boese, Kathy Polach, Ann Jury, Anne Lasser, Linda Cole, Leigh Ann Cole, Kim Clay, Claudia Martinez; third, Michelle Peterson, Nicole Jones, Kristen Peterson, Jenny Kreis, Jerry Zupancic, Deshonn Mabry, Derrick Clarke, Nikki Burkhardt, Liz Erio, Jennifer Skeldon, Marceline D'Oszno, Kim Mott, Felicia George, Michele Marquez, Christina Martinez, Annette Gannaway, Meghan Bruckert; fourth, Erika Dystrup, LaTonya Thompson, Josh Ryan, Mark Holm, Dexter Bonner, Joel Moore, Alvin Carroll, Eric Moorman, Aaron Kunze, Eli Limacher, Jeff Dahlen, Bill Zupancic, Geri Guardia, Ed Wood, Ronda Stokes, John Leslie, Timm Chaney, Dale Lasser, Paul Hacker, Josh Winter, Mike Zach; back, Matt Harmon, April Bazzio, Nuphul Mina, Zach Weber, Robert Boswell, Mike Magosky, Dave Turiciano, Rachel Gray, Jimmy Thomas, Greg Piskor, Bryan Ognizovich, Mike Tadey, Kevin Kaiser, Doug Kaiser, Robbie Lucas, Mike Phelan, Jeff Heine, Corey Grant, Rhonda Kiser, Dan Bohnert, Verna Toma.

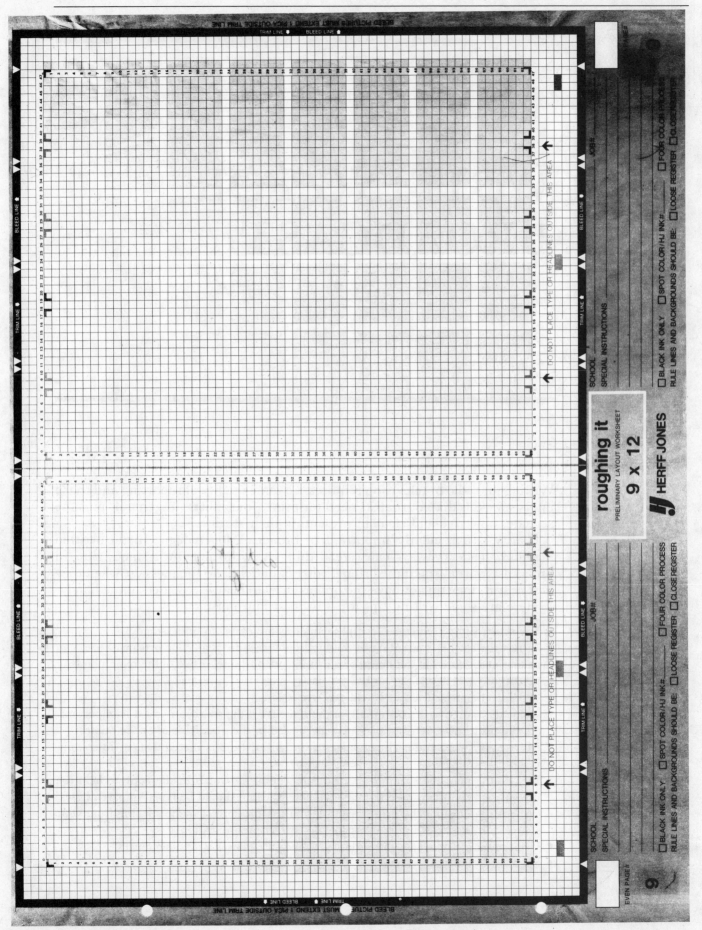

Courtesy of Joliet West (Illinois) Township High School *Yearbook*.

# CHAPTER FIFTEEN

# WRITING FOR BROADCAST

Writing for radio or television requires the same quality of reporting and sharp interview skills that journalists need for print. Journalists, in general, must be accuate, objective and clear in presenting their stories.

Clarity is particularly important in broadcast journalism. In the written medium, readers always can reread things they do not understand. But, in broadcast journalism, if the listeners do not understand the message when they first hear it, they do not have the opportunity to hear it repeated immediately.

Here are some writing tips for broadcast journalism:

- Use short, simple sentences. Simple sentences are easier to understand.
- Attract the listener's attention in the first sentence—the lead. The broadcast lead can be a brief summary of the news, or it can include just one or two of the main points in the story.
- Write in the present tense. Broadcasting is *now*.
- Name the source at the beginning of the sentence if the source involved is important. (In the print story, attribution is usually placed in the middle or after the quote.)
- Make every word count. In broadcast journalism, time is the equivalent to column inches.
- Include the phonetic spelling for names or confusing words in the copy to help the broadcaster say them correctly. The phonetic spelling should be typed in parentheses. (When you write for the print medium, you ask the correct name spelling from your sources. In broadcasting, you ask for the correct pronunciation.)
- Use commas, ellipses (. . .), or dashes to indicate pauses within sentences.
- Spell out numbers in your copy.

- Spell out "dollars" when referring to a specific amount. Print journalists write "$10." Broadcast journalists must write "ten dollars."
- Use caps and lowercase for your copy. All caps are harder to read.
- Double-space and time your copy; about 180 words equal one broadcast minute.

## Exercise 1

Below is an actual news story from the Associated Press, a wire service that provides news stories for newspapers. Rewrite this story for broadcast.

WASHINGTON (AP)—Wearing a wide grin, President Bush returned to work in the Oval Office on Monday as his heart resumed a normal rhythm under medication. "It's great to be back," he said after two nights in the hospital.

The success of the drug therapy allowed doctors to shelve plans to use an electrical shock procedure to make Bush's heart beat normally. The procedure would have required Bush to be put under a general anesthetic and to temporarily transfer power to Vice President Dan Quayle.

Bush's doctors recommended that he curtail his rigorous fitness regimen for a week or so while they fine-tune the drug dosages needed to keep his heartbeat stable. But they said Bush can resume his normal business schedule, and he went ahead with his appointments, including a meeting with former Soviet Foreign Minister Eduard Shevardnadze.

"Feel good," he said during a picture-taking session with Shevardnadze. With a sweep of his hands and a whistle, Bush indicated his heartbeat was normal.

"Talk to my doctor, will you?" he said, fending off further questions. "I'm just glad to be here." Bush, 66, appeared animated, though slightly tired.

"He can be expected to live the same life he was living last week," said Dr. Allan Ross, chief of cardiology at Georgetown University and a member of Bush's medical team.

Although Bush was responding to medication, his heart was still beating fast when he was discharged from Bethesda Naval Hospital, but it returned to normal shortly thereafter. Doctors said theyt hadn't been pressured to release him prematurely.

"It was a pure medical case without any decision having been made for political or other considerations," Dr. Burton Lee, Bush's personal physician, said in a news conference with other members of the medical team.

Lee said White House chief of staff John Sununu attended the meeting where doctors decided to release Bush but "didn't really do much more than listen."

The transfer of power from Bush to Quayle that had been envisioned could have caused political problems for the White House by focusing new attention on the qualifications of the vice president. Polls show that many Americans believe he is not qualified to be president.

Bush brushed aside questions about Quayle's competence. "Hey, he has my full support, always has, and he's doing a first-class job."

Although the immediate medical scare appeared over, doctors cautioned that Bush may again experience an irregular heartbeat as they make adjustments in his medications.

"It's really quite impossible so early in this go-round to firmly predict for you whether there'll ever be another episode," Ross said. "Certainly it's possible."

While Bush was described in good physical condition, Lee said, "He has said to me in the last couple of weeks, 'Gee-whiz, maybe I'm getting older.'" Lee said he discounted the remark because it was a hot day and "he was completely normal."

_____

_____

_____

_____

_____

_____

_____

_____

_____

_____

_____

_____

_____

_____

_____

_____

_____

_____

_____

## Exercise 2

Take a recent copy of your local newspaper and select 5 different news and sports stories. Clip only the first four paragraphs of each story. Then mount each clipping on the left side of a sheet of paper. Read the stories carefully. Then, again using the broadcast writing guidelines in the chapter introduction, write or type two or three sentences summarizing the story next to each clipping. Before you begin, identify the five stories you are using by writing their headlines below.

_____

_____

_____

_____

_____

# Exercise 3

Here is an actual UPI news story as it would appear in a newspaper. Rewrite it for your school's radio newscast.

Irving, Texas (UPI)—The PGA tour resumes its Texas swing Thursday at a new course which has the instant approval of Tom Watson.

"I really like it," said Watson, who heads the field for the Byron Nelson golf classic. But we are still feeling our way around it. It is sort of like being on a blind date.

The Nelson will be played on the tournament players' club—The Las Colinas Sports Club.

The par—70 layout, surrounded by spectator mounds, winds its way through native mesquite trees and is loaded with water hazards.

High winds of between 20 and 30 miles an hour could provide an instant test when the opening round is conducted Thursday.

"The course doesn't seem that long (6,767 yards)," Watson said. "But with the wind blowing, it is going to be difficult. There is some rough areas on the course, too, and when you combine that with the winds, you have an even tougher

Courtesy, United Press International, Inc.

golf course.

"I don't think this course favors anybody's game in particular. I think it just favors somebody who is playing real well. You have to keep the ball in play and you are going to have to putt good because these are very fast greens."

Watson came close to winning the first tour stop in Texas this year two weeks ago in Houston.

"I feel like my game is in good shape," said Watson, a four-time winner of the Nelson. "I think I'll have to putt a little better here to win . . . than I have been."

Bob Eastwood will be the defending champion this week, having won the third tournament of his career at the Nelson a year ago.

Eastwood went to the final tee last year three strokes behind Payne Stewart. But Eastwood birdied the final hole and Stewart double bogeyed it, forcing a playoff.

Eastwood bogeyed the first playoff hole, but Stewart suffered his second

double bogey in a row. Since that tournament Eastwood has had only one top 10 finish.

Despite the new course and despite the fact Nelson is one of the most beloved names in the game, this year's tournament has drawn a weaker than usual field.

Of the 15 players to have won a tournament on the tour this year only five are taking part—Hal Sutton, Bob Tway, Doug Tewell, Kenny Knox and Andy Bean. None of the winners from the past eight weeks are present.

Raymond Floyd will be among the featured players on hand, along with Lee Trevino, Lanny Wadkins, Ben Crenshaw, Craig Stadler and Nick Price, who last month broke the signal round record at the Masters with a 63.

Watson, the second leading money winner in the history of golf, needs a 16th place finish or better this week to surpass the $4 million mark in career earnings. Only Jack Nicklaus has won more ($4,836,384).

## Exercise 4

Here is a news story from The Associated Press as it would appear in print. Rewrite it for a televised broadcast.

Harrisburg, Pa. (AP)—Chrysler Corp. Chairman Lee Iacocca on Monday rejected an offer to fill Pennsylvania's vacant U.S. Senate seat, leaving Gov. Robert P. Casey still struggling to find an appointee.

"After lengthy discussions with my family and close friends, I concluded that I was not prepared to make the commitment necessary to fulfill the heavy responsibilities of a United States Senator," Iacocca said.

Chrysler spokesman A. C. Liebler said Casey offered the position to Iacocca last week, then visited the auto executive Thursday in Michigan.

Iacocca, 66, said he was flattered by the offer but was "looking forward to what I'll simply call a more 'normal' life." A native of Allentown, he has not resided in the state for years.

Iacocca votes in Michigan. To run for the seat, under the U.S. Constitution, he would have had to "inhabit" Pennsylvania at the time of the Nov. 5 special election. State election officials say an appointee would have to have a residence in the state at the time of the appointment.

Casey's office had no immediate comment on Iacocca's withdrawal. On Thursday, Casey denied that he had offered the job to anyone.

Despite Iacocca's decision, Democratic Party officials close to Casey said the governor will make his selection soon to fill a seat left vacant by the April 4 death of Republican John Heinz, who was killed in a plane-helicopter crash near Philadelphia.

"They're getting close but they're not ready to announce," one Democrat close to Casey said.

Sources who spoke on the condition of anonymity said former Philadelphia Mayor Bill Green is the apparent front-runner now, but Casey could still come up with a surprise.

Casey's selection process has been hindered by the decisions of several potential candidates against taking the job. They include U.S. Reps. Bill Gray of Philadelphia and John Murtha of Cambria County; Pittsburgh lawyer Art Rooney II; and Superior Court Judge Kate Ford Elliott.

The governor also has a problem with one candidate who wants the job, Lt. Gov. Mark Singel.

Casey has said he wants Singel to remain as his second-in-command, in part because a Republican, Senate President Pro Tem Robert Jubelirer, would become lieutenant governor if Singel went to the Senate.

Anne B. Anstine, chairman of the Republican State Committee, said Casey's handling of the Senate appointment "is embarrassing Pennsylvania."

"Was it really necessary for Governor Casey to fly to Detroit to recruit a senator for Pennsylvania?" she said in a statement.

While Casey is trying to make his choice, several would-be Republican candidates are waiting for U.S. Attorney General Dick Thornburgh to decide if he wants to run in the special election Nov. 5.

Others who are interested, including state Rep. Stephen Freind of Delaware County and U.S. Rep. Tom Ridge of Erie, said they would not run if Thornburgh does.

# Exercise 5

The following is a news story that appeared in the *Cedar Rapids Gazette* paper in Iowa. Rewrite the story in broadcast form.

# Iowa renews talk of multi-state lotto

By Judy Daubenmier
Gazette Des Moines Bureau

Des Moines—Iowa Lottery officials, with its new Lotto just barely off the ground, are again discussing with other states the prospect of a multi-state Lotto.

Lottery Commissioner Ed Stanek will be in New York today to meet with lottery officials from about eight states to discuss multi-state Lotto ideas.

The meeting, initially suggested by Rhode Island lottery officials, will be attended by officials of Rhode Island, Washington, D.C., New Hampshire and Delaware, among other states.

"The plan is not to sign contracts, but to talk about the idea, its pros and cons," Stanek said.

Several months ago, Stanek had discussed a multi-state lottery with officials in Nebraska and South Dakota, but those discussions have been at a standstill pending the passage of legislation or constitutional amendments in those states to permit that form of gambling.

Although there could be distribution and other problems with running interstate instant ticket games in widely scattered states, Stanek pointed out that when it comes to interstate agreements with computer-run games like Lotto, the state need not be limited to considering adjacent states.

"From a technical standpoint, as long as it's an on-line game like Lotto, it's not too much of a problem to operate a multi-state lottery. We could run a game with a colony on the moon as long as the communications system worked," he noted.

The attraction of multi-state Lottos to states like Iowa and Rhode Island is that bigger jackpots can be offered because there are more people to buy tickets.

But Stanek says there are drawbacks to that as well. Depending on the size of the population of the states Iowa joined with, the top prize likely wouldn't be won by Iowans each time. Statistically speaking, how often Iowans did win the top prize would depend on what percentage of the tickets Iowans bought. If Iowans bought only 10 percent of the tickets, odds are the jackpot would be won by an Iowan only 10 percent of the time.

That sort of situation has happened in the country's only Tri-State Lotto in Maine, Vermont and New Hampshire, Stanek noted. Vermont went 22 straight weeks without having one of its residents win the jackpot and then a Vermont resident won the single largest jackpot ever given in the game.

"We have to ask ourselves how peo-ple would react to that kind of game. I'm not sure (how Iowans would react)," Stanek said.

Today's meeting, he said, is a chance for officials interested in interstate lotteries to discuss what the ground rules for such enterprises should be.

Stanek also said he is planning future discussions with officials of the Missouri and Illinois lotteries about the possibility of joining with either one of them.

Discussions with Missouri, whose Lotto won't start until next year, have been hampered by the illness of its director.

In the case of Illinois, Stanek said "very preliminary" discussions have been held.

"At this time, I can't say there is a clear direction one way or the other" regarding Illinois' interest, he said.

"Illinois has to ask itself why it would participate other than to offer larger prizes. It has already given the largest prize to any individual in the country. They may not need it."

"Current thinking is that if an interstate Lotto should come into being, it would operate alongside the state's existing Lotto product.

For that reason, he said, Iowa might want to wait a while to make sure its new Lotto has "matured."

_____

_____

_____

_____

## Exercise 6

You are planning your school radio's newscast. Rewrite the following story that appeared in the *Des Moines Register* in Iowa.

# SAT error mars testing of seven Iowa students

By Mark Horstmeyer
Register Staff Writer

Seven Iowa high school juniors struggled through a college entrance examination Saturday for one hour and 50 minutes when they discovered their tests were no good.

They were among 7,500 students across the nation who found two blank pages on the mathematics test of the Scholastic Aptitude Tests. The math test was the fourth of six tests students complete. Each test takes about 30 minutes.

"It's got to be a big disappointment," said Bob Peterson, pupil services coordinator at Roosevelt High School, the Des Moines-area site for the national test.

Officials at Bettendorf High School, Cedar Rapids Washington High School and Luther College in Decorah—the other three Iowa test sites—said students testing there also encountered blank pages.

Two of the 190 students who took the SAT at Roosevelt found blank pages, two of 80 youngsters at Bettendorf had spoiled tests as did two of 91 students at Cedar Rapids.

The odds did not favor the only student who took the exam at Luther College. His test had the two blank pages.

The students with defective exams will be allowed to take the test again without charge. Students pay $11.50 to take the tests. Nationwide, about 300,000 high school juniors took the test Saturday.

Comparatively few Iowa students take the SAT because most Midwestern colleges require the American College Tests entrance exam.

"I've been here seven years and my colleague for 20 years, and we've never had this kind of thing happen. It's a monumental error," said Duane Buchheit, a counselor at Cedar Rapids Washington.

He said the two girls who had the defective test booklets "were very disappointed. They traveled from Cedar Falls and Waverly-Shell Rock."

The test will be given again June 7 at different sites. School officials said the students may take them then or wait until fall.

"We urge students to take them their junior year and again in the fall of their senior year," said Peterson, noting that the first time is to give students an idea of what the test is like.

_____

_____

_____

_____

_____

# Exercise 7

Here is another AP news story as it might appear in the newspaper: Assume you are a TV journalist. Write this story in newscast form.

WASHINGTON (AP)—Secretary of State James A. Baker III said Monday he expects to return to the Middle East later this week to renew his effort to set up a regional peace conference.

"As long as there is any reasonable prospect of any chance of success, we should continue to work at this," Baker said. The visit will be his fourth since a cease-fire was agreed to in the Persian Gulf War.

Baker, who returned from his most recent trip just 10 days ago, said the countries on his itinerary will be essentially the same as last time.

Baker disclosed his travel plans while welcoming former Soviet Foreign Minister Eduard Shevardnadze on a return visit to the State Department.

During his trip, Baker said he planned to visit with Shevardnadze's successor, Alexander Besmertnykh, to try to cordinate plans for a Middle East peace conference, which would be held under joint Soviet-American sponsorship.

Baker said the plan continues to call for direct talks between Israel and its Arab neighbors as well as face to face talks between Israel and Palestinian representatives.

Baker said the decision to go ahead with the trip was made following a telephone discussion with President Bush.

He and the president agreed, Baker said, that "we should continue to try."

During his most recent mission, Baker went to Israel, Egypt, Syria, Jordan, Saudi Arabia, Kuwait and the Soviet Union. The administration acknowledged afterward that the results of the mission were "slim."

No leader with whom Baker spoke rejected his proposals out of hand but all insisted on preconditions that have made many analysts wonder whether the plan has any realistic possibilities.

Baker maintained from the outset that the outcome of the Gulf War opened a "window of opportunity" for progress on the Arab-Israeli front that should not be squandered away.

Earlier, Shevardnadze proposed that worldwide sanctions be imposed against Middle Eastern countries that refuse to participate in direct peace talks.

"Many have claimed places at the table but do little to get the talks started," Shevardnadze said.

"We could apply sanctions to any country that refuses to negotiate directly" with other parties to a dispute that is before the United Nations Security Council, he suggested. He also proposed restricting arms shipments to the region to compel countries to end their arms race.

## Exercise 8

Obtain a copy of your school's latest newspaper. Assume that all of the news in the paper happened recently (yesterday or today). Select several stories on the basis of their importance and clip them. Mount each one on a separate sheet of paper. You are now ready to write a five-minute radio or TV newscast for your school. Using the guidelines introduced in this chapter, write a broadcast news summary for each story. Remember that 180 words equals one minute. Write the story titles (leads) below.

_____

_____

_____

_____

_____

_____

_____

_____

_____

# BRAINSTORMING TECHNIQUE

Brainstorming is a valuable technique that will help you gather ideas and information quickly. The method can be used in many situations. You and your colleagues can brainstorm for in-depth story topics, editorials, methods of increasing readership and even sources of advertisement for a special issue.

A typical brainstorming session follows these steps:

a. The problem, or goal for the session, is explained briefly by a group leader. If the school paper is publishing a special issue on the dangers of sports, the problem, or goal of the session, would be: What kinds of stories should be covered?

b. Everyone in the group should take two to three minutes to come up with several ideas.

c. All participants should have more than one idea in case their first idea is mentioned by someone else.

d. One at a time, each participant briefly proposes his or her idea.

e. All ideas are written down by a group recorder.

f. There can be *no* criticism or discussion of the ideas by any participant.

g. Once all the participants have offered their ideas, the group leader then can take ideas from anyone at random.

h. After ideas have been exhausted, the list is narrowed down.

i. Everyone in the group must select the top three or five best choices in order of importance and list them on a piece of paper. These choices are given to the group leader.

j. The votes are counted; the ideas are ranked.

k. Discussions or additional brainstorming, then can center on each of the top ideas.

Results of a brainstorming session can be noted on an outline, such as the one that follows.

# Brainstorming

Problem: _____ Round: _____ Date: _____

## Step I  Gather the Ideas:

1. _____
2. _____
3. _____
4. _____
5. _____
6. _____
7. _____
8. _____
9. _____
10. _____

11. _____
12. _____
13. _____
14. _____
15. _____
16. _____
17. _____
18. _____
19. _____
20. _____

## Step II  Personal Choices:

1. _____
2. _____
3. _____
4. _____
5. _____

## Step III  Group Consensus:

1. _____
2. _____
3. _____
4. _____
5. _____

## Step IV  Group Comments:

_____
_____

# APPENDIX
# B

## Copy Editing Symbols

| | |
|---|---|
| Indent for paragraph | L or ¶ |
| Insert a letter | . . . she told the crod . . . |
| Lower case | . . . he Ran with the ball . . . |
| Capitalize | . . . the student council also . . . |
| Delete and close up | . . . the student council also . . . |
| Delete and close up | . . . he ran with the the ball . . . |
| Delete and close up | . . . Tech won it's ninth title . . . |
| Abbreviate | . . . occurred at 9 No. 10th Street . . . |
| Delete and close up | . . . the life saving equipment . . . |
| Spell out | . . . 7 persons were arrested . . . |
| Insert a dash | . . . 17 persons all under 21 wore . . . |
| Set in numerals | . . . thirty-seven fled the scene . . . |
| Spell out | . . . the gov. Tuesday told . . . |
| Transpose letters | . . . the football coach said . . . |
| Insert a hyphen | . . . a well dressed person will . . . |
| Transpose words | . . . was also chosen . . . |
| Insert a word | . . . something was left out . . . |
| Separate words | . . . they arrived on Tuesday . . . |
| Insert period | . . . he said But Jones . . . |
| Insert comma | . . . never again she said . . . |
| Let it stand: ignore copy mark | . . . this is wrong . . . stet |
| Center | ]Copyright 1992[ |
| Set flush right | By the Associated Press ] |
| Set flush left | [By the Associated Press |
| No paragraph | . . . but not until then. no ¶ Later, however, she said . . . |
| Insert quotation marks | . . . Get out, he said . . . |
| Insert apostrophe | . . . its always like this . . . |